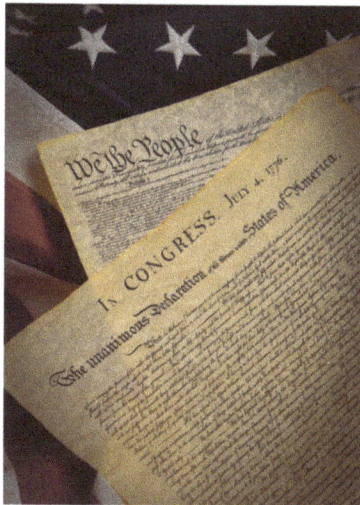

Books by Jaime Jackson

Equine

The Natural Horse: Lessons from the Wild (1992, rev. 2022)

Horse Owners Guide to Natural Hoof Care (1999)

Founder – Prevention and Cure the Natural Way (2001)

Guide To Booting Horses for Hoof Care Professionals (2002)

Paddock Paradise: A Guide to Natural Horse Boarding (2005)

The Natural Trim: Principles and Practice (2012)

The Healing Angle: Nature's Gateway to the Healing Field (2014)

Laminitis: An Equine Plague of Unconscionable Proportions (2016)

The Natural Trim: Basic Guidelines (2019)

The Natural Trim: Advanced Guidelines (2019, under revision)

Other

The Canvas Tipi (1982) Out of print.

Guard Your Teeth: Why the Dental Industry Fails Us – A Guide to Natural Dental Care (2018)

Buckskin Tanner: A Guide to Natural Hide Tanning (2019)

Cheyenne Tipi Notes: Technical Insights Into 19th Century Plains Indian Bison Hide Tanning (2019)

Zoo Paradise: A New Model for Humane Zoological Gardens (2019)

Living Behind the Facade: The Memoirs Of George E. Somers - A Gay Man's Journey Through the 20th Century (2019, rev. 2023)

Platform (2019, rev. 2024)

Horse Trek: Into the Mystic (2023, released 2024)

Platform

A Humanitarian Model For
An Egalitarian Society

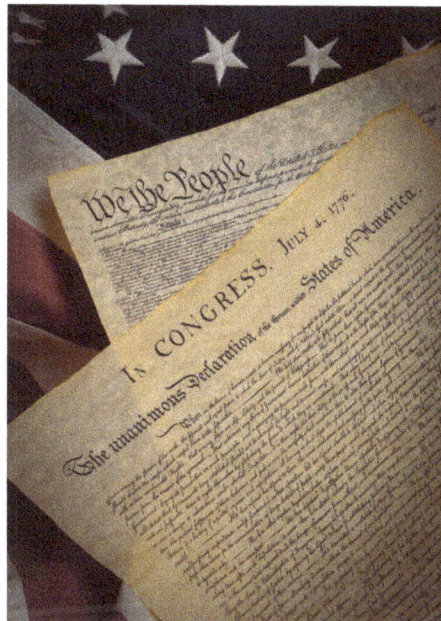

Jaime Jackson

NATURAL WORLD PUBLICATIONS

ISBN 978-1-7333094-5-5

Natural World Publications
P.O. Box 1765
Harrison, AR 72602-1765

www.naturalworldpublications.com
NaturalWorldPublications@gmail.com

I would unite with anybody to do right
and with nobody to do wrong.
— Frederick Douglass

Contents

Egalitarian Objectives (cont'd)

IN CONGRESS, JULY 4, 1776.

The unanimous Declaration of the thirteen united States of America.

When in the Course of human events, it becomes necessary for one people to dissolve the political bands which have connected them with another, and to assume among the powers of the earth, the separate and equal station to which the Laws of Nature and of Nature's God entitle them, a decent respect to the opinions of mankind requires that they should declare the causes which impel them to the separation.

We hold these truths to be self-evident, that all men are created equal, that they are endowed by their Creator with certain unalienable Rights, that among these are Life, Liberty and the pursuit of Happiness.—That to secure these rights, Governments are instituted among Men, deriving their just powers from the consent of the governed,—That whenever any Form of Government becomes destructive of these ends, it is the Right of the People to alter or to abolish it, and to institute new Government, laying its foundation on such principles and organizing its powers in such form, as to them shall seem most likely to effect their Safety and Happiness. Prudence, indeed, will dictate that Governments long established should not be changed for light and transient causes; and accordingly all experience hath shewn, that mankind are more disposed to suffer, while evils are sufferable, than to right themselves by abolishing the forms to which they are accustomed. But when a long train of abuses and usurpations, pursuing invariably the same Object evinces a design to reduce them under absolute Despotism, it is their right, it is their duty, to throw off such Government, and to provide new Guards for their future security.—Such has been the patient sufferance of these Colonies; and such is now the necessity which constrains them to alter their former Systems of Government. The history of the present King of Great Britain is a history of repeated injuries and usurpations, all having in direct object the establishment of an absolute Tyranny over these States. To prove this, let Facts be submitted to a candid world.

He has refused his Assent to Laws, the most wholesome and necessary for the public good.

He has forbidden his Governors to pass Laws of immediate and pressing importance, unless suspended in their operation till his Assent should be obtained; and when so suspended, he has utterly neglected to attend to them.

He has refused to pass other Laws for the accommodation of large districts of people, unless those people would relinquish the right of Representation in the Legislature, a right inestimable to them and formidable to tyrants only.

He has called together legislative bodies at places unusual, uncomfortable, and distant from the depository of their Public Records, for the sole purpose of fatiguing them into compliance with his measures.

He has dissolved Representative Houses repeatedly, for opposing with manly firmness his invasions on the rights of the people.

He has refused for a long time, after such dissolutions, to cause others to be elected; whereby the Legislative powers, incapable of Annihilation, have returned to the People at large for their exercise; the State remaining in the mean time exposed to all the dangers of invasion from without, and convulsions within.

He has endeavoured to prevent the population of these States; for that purpose obstructing the Laws for Naturalization of Foreigners; refusing to pass others to encourage their migrations hither, and raising the conditions of new Appropriations of Lands.

He has obstructed the Administration of Justice, by refusing his Assent to Laws for establishing Judiciary powers.

He has made Judges dependent on his Will alone, for the tenure of their offices, and the amount and payment of their salaries.

He has erected a multitude of New Offices, and sent hither swarms of Officers to harrass our people, and eat out their substance.

He has kept among us, in times of peace, Standing Armies without the Consent of our legislatures.

He has affected to render the Military independent of and superior to the Civil power.

He has combined with others to subject us to a jurisdiction foreign to our constitution, and unacknowledged by our laws; giving his Assent to their Acts of pretended Legislation:

For Quartering large bodies of armed troops among us:

For protecting them, by a mock Trial, from punishment for any Murders which they should commit on the Inhabitants of these States:

For cutting off our Trade with all parts of the world:

For imposing Taxes on us without our Consent:

For depriving us in many cases, of the benefits of Trial by jury:

For transporting us beyond Seas to be tried for pretended offences

For abolishing the free System of English Laws in a neighbouring Province, establishing therein an Arbitrary government, and enlarging its Boundaries so as to render it at once an example and fit instrument for introducing the same absolute rule into these Colonies:

For taking away our Charters, abolishing our most valuable Laws, and altering fundamentally the Forms of our Governments:

For suspending our own Legislatures, and declaring themselves invested with power to legislate for us in all cases whatsoever.

He has abdicated Government here, by declaring us out of his Protection and waging War against us.

He has plundered our seas, ravaged our Coasts, burnt our towns, and destroyed the lives of our people.

He is at this time transporting large Armies of foreign Mercenaries to compleat the works of death, desolation and tyranny, already begun with circumstances of Cruelty & perfidy scarcely paralleled in the most barbarous ages, and totally unworthy the Head of a civilized nation.

He has constrained our fellow Citizens taken Captive on the high Seas to bear Arms against their country, to become the executioners of their friends and Brethren, or to fall themselves by their Hands.

He has excited domestic insurrections amongst us, and has endeavoured to bring on the inhabitants of our frontiers, the merciless Indian Savages, whose known rule of warfare, is an undistinguished destruction of all ages, sexes and conditions.

In every stage of these Oppressions We have Petitioned for Redress in the most humble terms: Our repeated Petitions have been answered only by repeated injury. A Prince, whose character is thus marked by every act which may define a Tyrant, is unfit to be the ruler of a free people.

Nor have We been wanting in attentions to our British brethren. We have warned them from time to time of attempts by their legislature to extend an unwarrantable jurisdiction over us. We have reminded them of the circumstances of our emigration and settlement here. We have appealed to their native justice and magnanimity, and we have conjured them by the ties of our common kindred to disavow these usurpations, which, would inevitably interrupt our connections and correspondence. They too have been deaf to the voice of justice and of consanguinity. We must, therefore, acquiesce in the necessity, which denounces our Separation, and hold them, as we hold the rest of mankind, Enemies in War, in Peace Friends.

We, therefore, the Representatives of the united States of America, in General Congress, Assembled, appealing to the Supreme Judge of the world for the rectitude of our intentions, do, in the Name, and by Authority of the good People of these Colonies, solemnly publish and declare, That these United Colonies are, and of Right ought to be Free and Independent States; that they are Absolved from all Allegiance to the British Crown, and that all political connection between them and the State of Great Britain, is and ought to be totally dissolved; and that as Free and Independent States, they have full Power to levy War, conclude Peace, contract Alliances, establish Commerce, and to do all other Acts and Things which Independent States may of right do.—And for the support of this Declaration, with a firm reliance on the protection of divine Providence, we mutually pledge to each other our Lives, our Fortunes and our sacred Honor.

John Hancock

Button Gwinnett
Lyman Hall
Geo Walton.

Wm Hooper
Joseph Hewes,
John Penn

Edward Rutledge.

Thos Heyward Junr.
Thomas Lynch Junr.
Arthur Middleton

Robt Morris
Benjamin Rush
Benja. Franklin
John Morton
Geo Clymer
Jas. Smith.
Geo. Taylor
James Wilson
Geo. Ross
Caesar Rodney
Geo Read
Tho M:Kean

Samuel Chase
Wm Paca
Thos. Stone
Charles Carroll of Carrollton

George Wythe
Richard Henry Lee
Th Jefferson
Benja Harrison
Thos Nelson jr.
Francis Lightfoot Lee
Carter Braxton

Wm Floyd
Phil. Livingston
Frans Lewis
Lewis Morris

Richd Stockton
Jno Witherspoon
Fras Hopkinson
John Hart
Abra Clark

Josiah Bartlett
Wm Whipple
Saml Adams
John Adams
Robt Treat Paine
Elbridge Gerry
Step Hopkins
William Ellery
Roger Sherman
Sam el Huntington
Wm Williams
Oliver Wolcott
Matthew Thornton

Platform: A Humanitarian Model For An Egalitarian Society

Platform is about a humane, democratic process for egalitarian social change. Egalitarianism removes profiteering from the administering of vital essentials to its people. It encourages free enterprise and socialist instruments of economy — harnessed by egalitarian principles — to bring wealth to society as a whole, not to one class that dooms another to poverty. Also fundamental to this premise is that women must be accorded "equal status" under United States Constitutional law. They are not, and, thus, American society continues to dwell politically, economically, and socially in a quasi-democratic country with women accorded "2nd Class Status." *This must change if we are to prosper and survive as a genuine democratic society.*

Second class status also points directly at a new and virulent strain of postcolonial *feudalism* that has evolved in our country from its inception 243 years ago. At the founding of the nation, there was the *Old Feudalism*[1]: an institutionalized class society with a minority of white men accorded full Constitutional rights, and a majority of "lower classes" — that is, everyone else, including women, children, African slaves, and Native Americans — accorded few or no Constitutional rights, including the rights to vote and own property. The Old Feudalism over time then evolved into the *New Feudalism* that we live with today. The U.S. Constitution co-evolved too, but it still does not fully accord equal rights as not a majority of the States have ratified the Equal Rights Amendment. The result is a new class society comprised of a minority of billionaire (and soon to be trillionaire) industrialists, a lower wealthy class of multi-millionaires (sustainable incomes of more than $30 million dollars per year), a "middle class," followed by the poor, and then the homeless.

Platform holds that the middle class, the poor, and the homeless actually consti-

---

[1]The feudal systems presented here are modern variants of their 9th through 15th century medieval ("middle ages") variants. While historians are contentious over the actual defining characteristics of medieval feudal societies, *Platform* holds that they were all oppressive hierarchical forms of subservience of persons of lesser wealth ("vassals") catering to a higher entity of authority with greater wealth, typically a lord or king at the top, and involving use of land ("land tenure") in return for various forms of homage ("payback"). Humanity's natural inclination for egalitarianism reform brought medieval feudalism to an end, only to be replaced by new and often brutally ruthless political systems of class society that are discussed later in this book.

(*Facing page*) *United States Declaration of Independence.* Transcription is on page 82.

tute a single "mega-body" of impoverishment and despair that points to serious social, political, and economic inequities. The numbers of Americans living within this poverty zone are not exactly known, but most advocates for the poor are dubious of government data. There seems to be a consensus, however, that a somewhat annual shifting population of 37 to 43 million Americans, or approximately 13% of the U.S. population, live below the government's "poverty threshold" in recent years. That's more than the entire population of the State of California! But according to data published by the *Routledge Handbook of Poverty in the United States*, by including Americans living in "near-poverty" the number raises to a staggering 100 million, or a third of the entire U.S. population! This number corresponds to what *Platform* identifies above as the mega-body of people living in poverty.

The middle and lower classes are the least stable in our society. A vulnerable "middle class" of workers continues to slide towards the bottom as industrialists slash wages, eliminate benefits (e.g., healthcare), and hire part-time help, adding to the ranks of the poor at the lower threshold if they lose their jobs. Many jobs are lost altogether, such as when they are exported abroad to exploit other nationals desperate for work by paying them "slave" wages with few or no benefits. At the very bottom, our homeless men, women, parents with children, single women with children — and women of "color" in particular — are the most vulnerable and collectively suffer the most in a nightmare of behavioral dysfunction, poverty and despair. Without true egalitarian change, there is no way out of the bottom for the expanding "lower classes" in our society. Some may argue that jobs are the way out. But the inherent problems of this virulent strain of class society run much deeper than employment, compounded by the fact that the upper classes of the New Feudalism are arguably out of control themselves, due to an unrestrained profit motive and disdain for the poor. But what does this mean exactly?

The New Feudalism suggests that the lower classes are "destitute surplus populations in need of control and punishment" [Rutledge Handbook] deserved of their fate, and that the accumulation and islanding of wealth in the "upper classes" is the rightful, if not the inevitable, result of class privilege. *Platform* contends that this perspective is inherently immoral and reflects a toxic mentality rooted in our quasi-capitalist-socialist system. And further, that clearer thinking Americans ought to embrace and promote egalitarian principles at large so as to dismantle the New Feudalism and its apartheid system of the wealthy thriving on the misery and impoverishment of others. *Platform*, in contrast, is a concept for an egalitarian society, rather than a class society that inures to an acceptance of expanding poverty and human despair across the middle and lower classes, the "mega-body" of the New Feudalism.

Egalitarianism and Classism

While the focus of this book is the New Feudalism in the United States of America (USA), *Platform*, as a democratic egalitarian model for change, is applicable to any country unfortunately invested in a class society with an out of control and contracting upper class of the super wealthy atop an expansive and deepening lower class of the impoverished. *Egalitarianism, or more specifically, Democratic Egalitarianism, is a belief in human equality and opportunity especially with respect to the social, political, and economic lives of a nation's people.* Notwithstanding two caveats discussed below, it is rooted in the spirit of the second sentence of the U.S. Declaration of Independence:

> *We hold these truths to be self-evident, that all men are created equal, that they are endowed by their Creator with certain unalienable Rights, that among these are Life, Liberty and the pursuit of Happiness.*

In keeping with egalitarian principles, the term "all men" is to be interpreted as "all members of society"; and the pronouncement, "endowed by their Creator," is to be expanded to mean "endowed by their Creator and/or by Nature," in keeping with the Declaration's first sentence, "the Laws of Nature and of Nature's God entitle them," as clarified by the 1st Amendment to the U.S. Constitution, which states, "Congress shall make no law respecting an establishment of religion." *Platform* holds there should be no tyranny of religion or atheism, meaning, "My belief, my business; your belief, your business."

Egalitarianism is the moral and ethical alternative to class society, and it provides a logical and humane panacea for change. *Classism*, the antithesis of egalitarianism, is defined *as prejudice or discrimination based on one's class, which often also intersects with racialism.* Democratic Egalitarianism invites all philosophical and religious perspectives that address such inequities, from evangelical to atheist. For example, the self-avowed anarchist and atheist, Alexander Berkman (1870 - 1936) espoused an important characterization of egalitarianism in his pamphlet, *What is Anarchism?*, published in 1927:

Alexander Berkman — leading member of the anarchist movement in the early 20th century.

"Equality does not mean an equal amount but equal opportunity . . . It does not mean that every one must eat, drink, or wear the same things, do the same work, or live in the same manner. Far from it: the very reverse in fact . . . Individual needs and tastes differ, as appetites differ. It is equal opportunity to satisfy them that constitutes true equality . . . Far from leveling, such equality opens the door for the greatest possible variety of activity and development. For human character is diverse. "

§

Christians for Biblical Equality (CBE) is a predominantly evangelical egalitarian organization headquartered in Minneapolis, Minnesota. Their core values, published in 2018, state:

1. Scripture is our authoritative guide for faith, life, and practice.

2. Patriarchy (male dominance) is not a biblical ideal but a result of sin.

3. Patriarchy is an abuse of power, taking from females what God has given them: their dignity, and freedom, their leadership, and often their very lives.

4. While the Bible reflects patriarchal culture, the Bible does not teach patriarchy in human relationships.

5. Christ's redemptive work frees all people from patriarchy, calling women and men to share authority equally in service and leadership.

6. God's design for relationships includes faithful marriage between a man and a woman, celibate singleness and mutual submission in Christian community.

7. The unrestricted use of women's gifts is integral to the work of the Holy Spirit and essential for the advancement of the gospel in the world.

8. Followers of Christ are to oppose injustice and patriarchal teachings and practices that marginalize and abuse females and males.

§

Members of the CBE weren't the only Christians protesting women's 2nd class status. In 2009, U.S. President Jimmy Carter (born 1924, "James Earl Carter Jr.") published the following profound open letter, which he entitled, "Losing my religion for equality":

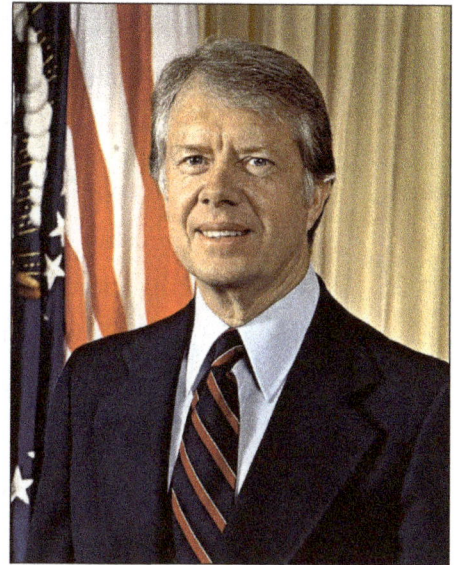

Jimmy Carter — 39th president of the United States.

Women and girls have been discriminated against for too long in a twisted interpretation of the word of God.

I have been a practicing Christian all my life and a deacon and Bible teacher for many years. My faith is a source of strength and comfort to me, as religious beliefs are to hundreds of millions of people around the world. So my decision to sever my ties with the Southern Baptist Convention, after six decades, was painful and difficult. It was, however, an unavoidable decision when the convention's leaders, quoting a few carefully selected Bible verses and claiming that Eve was created second to Adam and was responsible for original sin, ordained that women must be "subservient" to their husbands and prohibited from serving as deacons, pastors or chaplains in the military service.

This view that women are somehow inferior to men is not restricted to one religion or belief. Women are prevented from playing a full and equal role in many faiths. Nor, tragically, does its influence stop at the walls of the church, mosque, synagogue or temple. This discrimination, unjustifiably attributed to a Higher Authority, has provided a reason or excuse for the deprivation of women's equal rights across the world for centuries.

At its most repugnant, the belief that women must be subjugated to the wishes of men excuses slavery, violence, forced prostitution, genital mutilation and national laws that omit rape as a crime. But it also costs many millions of girls and women control over their own bodies and lives, and continues to deny them fair access to education, health, employment and influence within their own communities.

The impact of these religious beliefs touches every aspect of our lives. They help explain why in many countries boys are educated before girls;

why girls are told when and whom they must marry; and why many face enormous and unacceptable risks in pregnancy and childbirth because their basic health needs are not met.

In some Islamic nations, women are restricted in their movements, punished for permitting the exposure of an arm or ankle, deprived of education, prohibited from driving a car or competing with men for a job. If a woman is raped, she is often most severely punished as the guilty party in the crime.

The same discriminatory thinking lies behind the continuing gender gap in pay and why there are still so few women in office in the West. The root of this prejudice lies deep in our histories, but its impact is felt every day. It is not women and girls alone who suffer. It damages all of us. The evidence shows that investing in women and girls delivers major benefits for society. An educated woman has healthier children. She is more likely to send them to school. She earns more and invests what she earns in her family.

It is simply self-defeating for any community to discriminate against half its population. We need to challenge these self-serving and out-dated attitudes and practices — as we are seeing in Iran where women are at the forefront of the battle for democracy and freedom.

Nelson R. Mandela — 1st President of South Africa.

I understand, however, why many political leaders can be reluctant about stepping into this minefield. Religion, and tradition, are powerful and sensitive areas to challenge. But my fellow Elders and I, who come from many faiths and backgrounds, no longer need to worry about winning votes or avoiding controversy — and we are deeply committed to challenging injustice wherever we see it.

The Elders are an independent group of eminent global leaders, brought together by former South African president Nelson Rolihlahla Mandela (1918 – 2013), who offer their influence and experience to support peace building, help address major causes of human suffering and promote the shared interests of humanity. We have decided to draw particular attention to the responsibility of religious and traditional leaders in ensuring equality and human rights and have recently published a statement that declares: "The justification of discrimination against women and girls on grounds of religion or tradition, as if it were prescribed by a Higher Authority, is unacceptable."

We are calling on all leaders to challenge and change the harmful teachings and practices, no matter how ingrained, which justify discrimination against women. We ask, in particular, that leaders of all religions have the courage to acknowledge and emphasize the positive messages of dignity and equality that all the world's major faiths share.

The carefully selected verses found in the Holy Scriptures to justify the superiority of men owe more to time and place - and the determination of male leaders to hold onto their influence - than eternal truths. Similar biblical excerpts could be found to support the approval of slavery and the timid acquiescence to oppressive rulers.

I am also familiar with vivid descriptions in the same Scriptures in which women are revered as pre-eminent leaders. During the years of the early Christian church women served as deacons, priests, bishops, apostles, teachers and prophets. It wasn't until the fourth century that dominant Christian leaders, all men, twisted and distorted Holy Scriptures to perpetuate their ascendant positions within the religious hierarchy.

The truth is that male religious leaders have had — and still have — an option to interpret holy teachings either to exalt or subjugate women. They have, for their own selfish ends, overwhelmingly chosen the latter. Their continuing choice provides the foundation or justification for much of the pervasive persecution and abuse of women throughout the world. This is in clear violation not just of the Universal Declaration of Human Rights but also the teachings of Jesus Christ, the Apostle Paul, Moses and the prophets, Muhammad, and founders of other great religions — all of whom have called for proper and equitable treatment of all the children of God. It is time we had the courage to challenge these views.

Classism and Welfare: Institutionalized Poverty and Homelessness

As stated, in the U.S. there is a shrinking "upper class" of super wealthy individuals,[1] who sit above in every respect — socially, politically, and economically — a spiraling and swelling "under class" of poor and homeless. The notion of being labeled "poor" or "homeless" strikes terror in the heart of every American, particularly in the "middle class" whose economic vulnerability is often repeated in the well-known muse of being "a single paycheck away from living in one's car or in the street." This descent towards and into the lowest classes is both humiliating to the human spirit and compromising of one's vitality. It also beckons and feeds the Darwinian social pathology of "survival of the fittest," including getting ahead at another's expense for whatever reason, typically an amalgamation of fear and greed. Like cancer, *poverty — the inability to make ends meet on one's own* — has become a ubiquitous and metastasizing socioeconomic disease spreading wherever severe economic depression renders people vulnerable, if not expendable by political default in the New Feudalism.

Arguably, and perhaps ironically so, poverty in America has become institutionalized. The problems of the under classes (those below the wealthy classes) are endemic to their population; however, their ubiquity in various forms threaten society as a whole (e.g., gang violence, drug trafficking, drug abuse, crime, mass murder, and proliferation of contagious and communicable diseases among the homeless). Thus, it is no surprise that our American capitalist system has necessarily acquired socialist instruments to try to deal with the burgeoning lower classes. Ever since the New Deal, the epithetical "welfare state" has grown and grown, much to the chagrin of the politically conservative "right" that holds the political left responsible for what they label pejoratively as "unnecessary entitlement programs" that encourage welfarism. As the political (liberal) left petitions

---

[1]While their population is shrinking relative to the total world's population, their concentration of wealth is inversely proportional. "The Global Wealth Report, which Boston Consulting Group (BCG) published in June 2014 in Washington, D.C., shows that liquid wealth of the super-rich, the Ultra-High-Net-Worth Households, had increased by 20% in 2013. BCG uses a household definition of UHNW which places only those with more than $100 million liquid financial wealth into the UHNW-category, more than the usual $30 million, with which the ultra-category had been created in 2007. According to BCG about 15,000 households globally belong in this group of the super-rich. They control 5.5% of global financial wealth. 5000 of them live in the US, followed by China, Britain and Germany. BCG expects the trend toward more concentrated wealth to continue unabated. While financial wealth of the sub-millionaires is expected to increase by 3.7% annually until 2019, the expected growth rate for the super-rich is 9.1%. The share of this group in global financial wealth would thus increase % to 6.5% by 2019." [https://en.wikipedia.org/wiki/Ultra_high-net-worth_individual#Billionaire_Census]

Senators Responsiveness to Income Groups

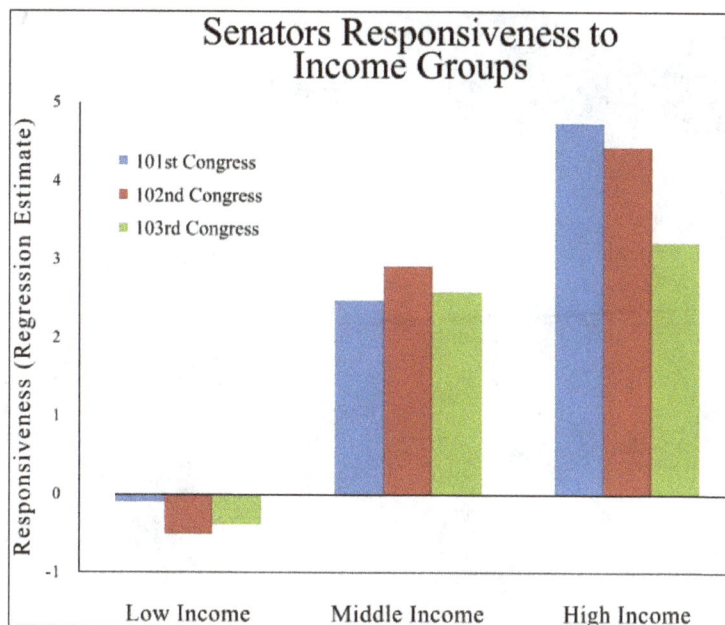

for more or expanded entitlements, the disgruntled political system inevitably has become more and more toxic, alienating many voters and striking terror in the dependent lower classes, while marginalizing the homeless further and further. Politicians are placed in the difficult, if not impossible, position of having to deal with growing poverty while serving the special interests of the upper classes (*table, above*).

Federal and state government programs of welfare relief (also referred to as "public assistance") were first created during the "New Deal" administration of President Franklin Delano Roosevelt (1882–1945). They have expanded considerably since then, and the disguised intent has always been to help the destitute, the elderly, and the disabled, with the basic things needed to live: shelter, food, and income. Indeed, at surface, these programs appear to have made a crucial and welcomed difference in the lives of the impoverished. To a certain extent, this assistance has even enabled some to rise into the middle classes and escape total dependence on government assistance programs. However, a more accurate characterization is

Franklin D. Roosevelt — 32nd President of the United States.

that there is a fluctuating "up and down" mobility between the middle class and the poor, the stability of which is based one's ability or capacity to obtain and secure employment or government assistance. Those more able to obtain work for any given period of time and also access entitlement programs, are less likely to descend

Homeless man sleeping across the street from the Colorado State Capitol Building in Denver.

into temporary homelessness, than those less capable of providing for themselves such as destitute drug addicts, convicted felons, the mentally disabled, and single women with children. In fact, these programs have done nothing to impede the architecture of the New Feudalism, because they were planned that way. They continue to favor the upper classes and send more Americans into poverty, an important focus of this book.

Indeed, evidence abounds for this orchestrated outcome. The expendable middle class, in particular, has been targeted for poverty by America's industrial feudalists. According to Allan N. Schwartz, LCSW, Ph.D., of the Gulf Bend Center that deals with mental health and substance abuse issues, an investigation done by the Johns Hopkins Behavioral Sciences and Psychiatry Department indicates there has been "a significant increase in the rates of suicide among white middle class men and women in the United States." He adds, "The rate of increase is especially high for women in this age group . . . the middle age group is considered to range from 36 to 65 years of age." It is thought this is due to depression and severe prescription drug abuse, but *Platform* holds that alienation from society and economic instability are at the bottom of it all.

Beneath the middle income classes, the destitute among us increasingly find

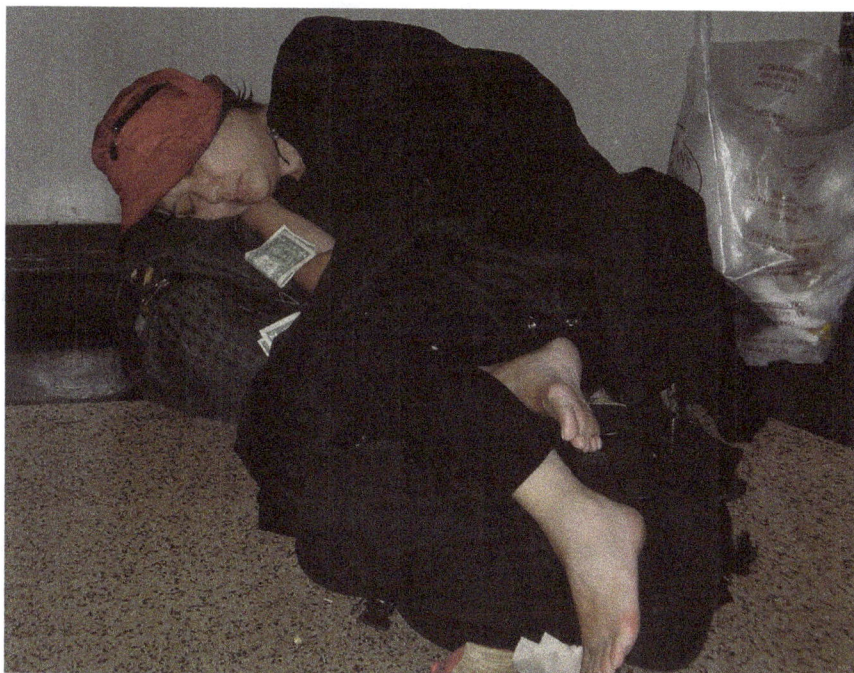

Women and families represent the fastest growing groups of the homeless popula-tion in the United States. *A national disgrace.*

themselves entrapped in permanent homelessness. The U.S. Department of Hous-ing and Urban Development's 2018 Annual Homeless Assessment Report, states that there are 530,000 thousand homeless Americans. In Los Angeles alone, 50,000 or more are homeless. Advocacy groups for the homeless claim that the numbers of homeless are actually much greater, with many more in the middle and lower classes teetering precariously on the brink of joining them at one time or another, if not permanently. I have not seen it myself, but was told by a Califor-nia law enforcement officer that over 200,000 homeless in his district are camped along a single major California river descending from the Sierra Nevada with no-where else to go. Homeless "tribes" have been reported moving from the outskirts of unwelcoming cities into nearby uninhabited desert lands in Arizona and New Mexico. It is well-known, too, that homeless camps of Latinos and nationals from other countries also numbering in the hundreds of thousands lie just across the U.S. southern border, most hopeful that one day they can find passage into the U.S. to find sanctuary from poverty (and often violence) in their own countries. Whether to allow them and others to enter the country, or to build a wall to keep them out, has become a major political battleground in the U.S. Congress today, and one that has also divided the American people, typically along political party lines.

The lack of affordable housing is arguably the greatest contributing factor to poverty in the U.S. The "housing crisis" can actually trace its roots back to the 1950s, 60s and 70s when it was discovered that homes could be sold at a profit, a new form of "upward mobility." For example, a very nice home purchased after WWII for five to ten thousand dollars, and affordable for the working middle class, may sell for half a million to a million or more today in parts of many states. But the overall effect has been to drive real estate prices higher and higher everywhere. In the present, affordable homes are increasingly scarce, forcing many to rent or fall into the ranks of the poor living in poverty, or into homelessness.

According to one report posted on Huffington Post, the National Low Income Housing Coalition has found that the multitudes earning the national minimum wage salary of $7.25 cannot afford to rent a modest 1 to 2 bedroom apartment in any of the 50 states. People living below the "poverty line" established by government statistics can't afford to rent anything and depend on public housing in one form of another and other public assistance programs to survive and avoid homelessness. While government statistics show that the majority of Americans, approximately 65%, live in homes they have purchased, most live in enormous debt, and nearly 70% are still carrying mortgages. Foreclosures are also high across this population.

What was once affordable home ownership has, thus, become a type of pyramid scheme roiling completely out of control. Investors from the upper and lower upper classes now control many rentals nationwide, and they will charge what they can get. One such investor I knew about owned over 1,000 homes by 1970 in East and West Oakland, California. Homes ghettoized by poverty and crime can today be purchased at 1950's or 60's prices, and then turned around and rented for current unaffordable rates to the poor when the owners use Section 8 to get from taxpayers that which they can't get from the poor! In some cities, as poverty struck entire neighborhoods, violence and crime made viable home ownership, and even renting, problematic. Homes were simply abandoned or became the instruments of "slum lording." Those lacking upkeep and occupation might be torn down due to city ordinances. Others became public housing units. More recently I have witnessed what appears to be a concerted and cooperative effort by rental agencies to raise rents high enough that the poor cannot afford anything. And, similarly, to

Hidden Hills is a city and gated community in Los Angeles County, California. It is located next to the city of Calabasas and is located in the west San Fernando Valley. It is notable for being home to many actors and celebrities, and others of the "lower upper classes."

the same end, to require income data and criminal background checks in their rental applications. This is tantamount to weaponizing rental requirements against the poor, in the same way that literacy tests have been weaponized against poor whites and blacks to prevent them from voting. Low or no income and a poor education are the weapons of discrimination against the poor in the New Feudalism.

All of this is in stark contrast to the upper ends of our class society, where "dream homes" and safe neighborhoods with 24 hour paid security patrols advertise "armed response" to protect person and property. Those who can afford it, move into gated communities with sentries culling or allowing those seeking passage. Like higher level politicians, the super rich of the upper classes have their own personal security detachments who go with them everywhere. The super rich — the industrialists — are also joined by famous rock stars and entertainers, all of whom typically have multiple homes, even their own private lake or island estates at sea with their own personal jets, helicopters, and million dollar yachts to ferry them to and fro. They are a closed society. This classist segregation of the "rich" from the "poor" characterizes the New Feudalism.

Historical context

Poverty is not new in the world and political revolutions have arisen to deal with it for centuries. More recently, such terms as communism, Marxism, socialism, fascism, anarchism, Maoism, and so forth, are now familiar — if not from education, then by name — to many, maybe most, Americans, certainly of the Vietnam War generation. These were, and still persist in variant forms as efforts by governments to deal with "class society" through egalitarian principles in some measure, but more often by indoctrination, coercion, violence, and even mass murder. On the egalitarian side, some of their economic objectives even sound good to many Americans, promising free education, health care, land ownership reform, jobs, and so on. But, as all of these were borne structurally with their own forms of class hierarchy, egalitarianism invariably gave way to oppressive regimes with dictatorial leaders, aloof political parties, secret police, militarism, and purported reforms that, in fact, tyrannically forced oppressed lower classes to do as their told (e.g., forced labor and military conscription), or face harsh consequences, including genocide (for example, the violent suppression of rival political groups by Bolsheviks during the Russian Revolution.).

Here at home, Americans once struggled under British colonialism, giving rise to the American Revolutionary War, which eventually led to the birth of the nation. Leaders of the revolution envisioned a new democratic state with elected officials answerable to the people. The concept was attractive to enough of the "rebel minded" (but thought by some to constitute no more than 3% of the colonial population) to put their lives on the line to defeat and throw out the British. While the American Declaration of Independence promised liberty, freedom, and justice for all, and that "all men are created equal," its authors had a very limited interpretation of who that applied to. One could argue that they really had themselves in mind, literally: white men who owned property. Everyone else was out. That contradiction meant things would go on as usual with human slavery, the slave trade out of Africa, male ownership of the land, the right to vote a privilege of white male landowners, a wealthy upper class, child labor, profitable militarism, the birth of banks, and so forth. In other words, institutionalization of a new aristocratic "class society" extruded right out of colonialism. Not everyone was happy about this outcome, to say the least.

Obviously, the "sounds good" concept of "freedom, equality, and justice for all" didn't sit well with women, African slaves, and Native Americans among others, who were left out of the deal. Creation of the U.S. Constitution with its Bill of Rights (and its eventual many Amendments) became a necessity from the beginning, if not to make things clear to those being excluded, certainly to protect the rights of the "chosen" elite — white male landowners. It then comes as no surprise that the War of 1812 found freed and runaway slaves manning the cannons on British ships bombing Washington, and whose "rocket's red glare," is so indelibly written in our country's national anthem![1] In a twist, the British had banned slavery by then, and one could argue that the American homeland defense was — much to the chagrin of American abolitionists — as much in defense of human slavery as anything else inuring to white male property owners in the new class society of the Old Feudalism.

Almost from the beginning, American women began to mobilize against their new "2nd Class Status," as did the anti-slavery abolitionists and those who opposed an emerging industrialized militarism. Freedom and equal rights, including citizenship and the right to vote, were the battle cry. Could white male privilege hold out against it? It would be difficult, but not impossible. In their favor was that every institution created in government was envisioned and created by white men: a Congress to write and pass the laws or legal mandates sent to the states for ratification; the courts that would interpret, defend, modify, or reject the Constitutionality of the laws; a militia to enforce the laws or rebellions. All that was needed was ratification by the States to keep things in check. But with only white males doing the voting and controlling the legal apparatus of both federal and state jurisdictions, it was a done deal. Women were kept out.

Dred Scott — denied freedom from slavery by the U.S. Constitution.

But so were slaves, freed-slaves, and any person identified as a black African-American. This was confirmed by the Supreme Court in their infamous 1857 *Dred Scott versus Sanford* decision, which modern lawyers and scholars all agree, was the "very worst of the worst of the court's decisions." The court was comprised of seven white males, of which two actually dissented the majority opinion. One — Benjamin Robbins Curtis, an anti-slavery advocate — subsequently resigned from the court in disgust. Chief Justice Roger Taney wrote for the majority:

---

[1]Not surprising. The phrase 'the hireling and slave' from the third stanza of the Star Spangled Banner has come under considerable scrutiny of late. According to British historian Robin Blackburn, the phrase alludes to the thousands of ex-slaves in the British ranks organized as the Corps of Colonial Marines, who had been liberated by the British and demanded to be placed in the battle line "where they might expect to meet their former masters.' In November 2017, the California Chapter of the NAACP called on Congress to remove "The Star-Spangled Banner" as the national anthem. Alice Huffman, California NAACP president said: "it's racist; it doesn't represent our community, it's anti-black."

We think . . . that [black people] are not included, and were not intended to be included, under the word "citizens" in the Constitution,
and can therefore claim none of the rights and privileges which that
instrument provides for and secures to citizens of the United States.
On the contrary, they were at that time [of America's founding] considered as a subordinate and inferior class of beings who had been
subjugated by the dominant race, and, whether emancipated or not,
yet remained subject to their authority, and had no rights or privileges but such as those who held the power and the Government
might choose to grant them.

Taney then used the U.S. Constitution to justify his opinion, writing:

Now, . . . the right of property in a slave is distinctly and expressly af-
firmed in the Constitution . . . Upon these considerations, it is the
opinion of the court that the act of Congress which prohibited a citizen from holding and owning property of this kind in the territory of
the United States north of the [36°N 36' latitude] line therein mentioned, is not warranted by the Constitution, and is therefore void.[1]

Native Americans during the American Revolutionary War were divided
amongst themselves as to whom to place their allegiance: the British or the rebel
American patriots. But it was actually a *Hobson's choice.* Siding with the British
targeted them as enemy combatants of the patriots, for which there would be severe reprisals if the rebels prevailed in gaining their independence. Putting in
with the revolting colonists, whether they prevailed or not, had its own uncertain-
ties including the likelihood that Americans would dislodge them from their
lands anyway. Many died in battles and on both sides, but in the end were forced

---

[1]Taney is referring to the Missouri Compromise. This was the legislation that provided for the admission of
Maine to the United States as a free state along with Missouri as a slave state, thus maintaining the balance of
power between North and South in the United States Senate. Thus slavery was prohibited north of the 36°30'
parallel, excluding Missouri. Congress passed the legislation on March 3, 1820, and President James Monroe
signed it on March 6, 1820. However, it was later repealed by the Kansas-Nebraska Act of 1854 which sought
to open up new territories in the recent Louisiana Purchase. But those territories would become anti-slavery as
provided by the Missouri Compromise. To appease pro-slavery legislators in Congress the Missouri Compromise was repealed as part of the legislation signed by anti-abolitionist President Franklin Pierce. This outraged
Northerners leading to new fighting and bloodshed between opposing forces in the new territories. These
tensions eventually led to the Civil War. The act also had adverse effects on Native Americans still living in
the territories, including devastating diseases and plagues brought by new pro and anti-slavery settlers as they
poured into the region.

"Trail of Tears."

The Trail of Tears was a consequence of the 1830 Indian Removal Act. Growing pressure from settlers encroaching on treaty lands led to the Act. It was a series of forced relocations occurring between from 1830 to 1838. Native Americans were escorted by the U.S. Army from their ancestral homelands in the Southeastern United States, to areas west of the Mississippi River that had been designated as Indian Territory. This included the Chickasaw, Choctaw, Creek, Seminole, and Cherokee people (including mixed-race and black slaves who lived among them). Thousands died from disease, exposure, starvation, forced marches, and violence perpetrated by frontiersmen along the way. President Jackson defended the relocation as a benefit to the Indians, writing,

> It will separate the Indians from immediate contact with settlements of whites; free them from the power of the States; enable them to pursue happiness in their own way and under their own rude institutions; will retard the progress of decay, which is lessening their numbers, and perhaps cause them gradually, under the protection of the Government and through the influence of good counsels, to cast off their savage habits and become an interesting, civilized, and Christian community.

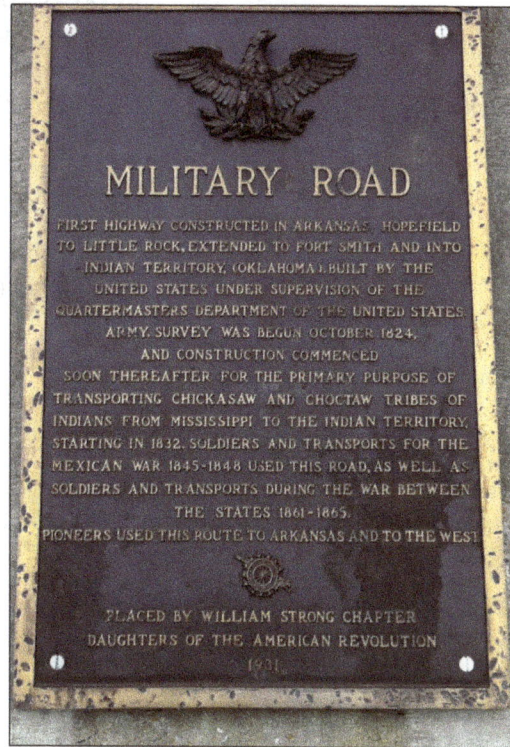

Historic Marker in Marion, Arkansas, denoting the "Trail of Tears."

to give up their lands. Later, the 1830 Indian Removal Act signed by President Andrew Jackson[1] (1767 – 1845) facilitated a forced military removal of Indian nations in the Southeastern United States to the west, what became Indian Territory, later Oklahoma Territory, and finally the State of Oklahoma in 1907.

By the 1890s, most Plains Indians and others further west were militarily confined to America's "Indian Reservations," and, not surprisingly, denied full citizenship until passage of the 1924 Snyder Act (also known as the Indian Citizenship Act), although not all states chose to comply. Further, the courts ruled that "according an Indian citizenship does not necessarily imply they also had the right to vote."

Not to be restrained, however, the first women's rights convention was organized at Seneca Falls, New York, in 1848. But no black

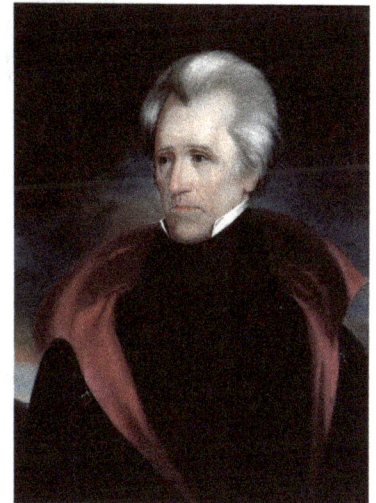

Andrew Jackson — 7th President of the United States.

[1]Jackson was an unrepentant slave owner and slave trader before, during, and after his presidency. He owned as many as 300 slaves, and ordered his overseers to use whippings to "increase productivity" and quell trouble.

Declaration of Sentiments[*]

When, in the course of human events, it becomes necessary for one portion of the family of man to assume among the people of the earth a position different from that which they have hitherto occupied, but one to which the laws of nature and of nature's God entitle them, a decent respect to the opinions of mankind requires that they should declare the causes that impel them to such a course.

We hold these truths to be self-evident: that all men and women are created equal; that they are endowed by their Creator with certain inalienable rights; that among these are life, liberty, and the pursuit of happiness; that to secure these rights governments are instituted, deriving their powers from the consent of the governed. Whenever any form of government becomes destructive of these rights, it is the right of those who suffer from it to refuse allegiance to it, and to insist upon the institution of a new government, laying its foundation on such principles, and organizing its powers in such form, as to them shall seem most likely to effect their safety and happiness.

Prudence, indeed, will dictate that governments long established should not be changed for light and transient causes; and accordingly all experience hath shown that mankind are more disposed to suffer, while evils are sufferable, than to right themselves by abolishing the forms to which they are accustomed, but when a long train of abuses and usurpations, pursuing invariably the same object, evinces a design to reduce them under absolute despotism, it is their duty to throw off such government, and to provide new guards for their future security. Such has been the patient sufferance of the women under this government, and such is now the necessity which constrains them to demand the equal station to which they are entitled.

The history of mankind is a history of repeated injuries and usurpation on the part of man toward woman, having in direct object the establishment of an absolute tyranny over her. To prove this, let facts be submitted to a candid world.

Having deprived her of this first right as a citizen, the elective franchise, thereby leaving her without representation in the halls of legislation, he has oppressed her on all sides.

- He has made her, if married, in the eye of the law, civilly dead.

- He has taken from her all right in property, even to the wages she earns.

- He has made her morally, an irresponsible being, as she can commit many crimes with impunity, provided they be done in the presence of her husband. In the covenant of marriage, she is compelled to promise obedience to her husband, he becoming, to all intents and purposes, her master—the law giving him power to deprive her of her liberty, and to administer chastisement.

- He has so framed the laws of divorce, as to what shall be the proper causes of divorce, in case of separation, to whom the guardianship of the children shall be given; as to be wholly regardless of the happiness of the women—the law, in all cases, going upon a false supposition of the supremacy of a man, and giving all power into his hands.

- After depriving her of all rights as a married woman, if single and the owner of property, he has taxed her to support a government which recognizes her only when her property can be made profitable to it.

- He has monopolized nearly all the profitable employments, and from those she is permitted to follow, she receives but a scanty remuneration.

- He closes against her all the avenues to wealth and distinction, which he considers most honorable to himself. As a teacher of theology, medicine, or law, she is not known.

- He has denied her the facilities for obtaining a thorough education—all colleges being closed against her.

- He allows her in church, as well as State, but a subordinate position, claiming Apostolic authority for her exclusion from the ministry, and, with some exceptions, from any public participation in the affairs of the Church.

- He has created a false public sentiment by giving to the world a different code of morals for men and women, by which moral delinquencies which exclude women from society, are not only tolerated but deemed of little account in man.

- He has usurped the prerogative of Jehovah himself, claiming it as his right to assign for her a sphere of action, when that belongs to her conscience and her God.

- He has endeavored, in every way that he could to destroy her confidence in her own powers, to lessen her self-respect, and to make her willing to lead a dependent and abject life.

Now, in view of this entire disfranchisement of one-half the people of this country, their social and religious degradation—in view of the unjust laws above mentioned, and because women do feel themselves aggrieved, oppressed, and fraudulently deprived of their most sacred rights, we insist that they have immediate admission to all the rights and privileges which belong to them as citizens of these United States.

In entering upon the great work before us, we anticipate no small amount of misconception, misrepresentation, and ridicule; but we shall use every instrumentality within our power to effect our object. We shall employ agents, circulate tracts, petition the State and national Legislatures, and endeavor to enlist the pulpit and the press in our behalf. We hope this Convention will be followed by a series of Conventions, embracing every part of the country.

---

*According to Tammy L. Brown, Associate Professor of Black World Studies, History, and Global and Intercultural Studies, Miami University, When suffragists gathered in Seneca Falls, New York, in July 1848, they advocated for the right of white women to vote. The participants were middle and upper-class white women, a cadre of white men supporters and one African-American male — Frederick Douglass. The esteemed abolitionist had forged a strong working relationship with fellow abolitionists and white women suffragists, including Elizabeth Cady Stanton and Susan B. Anthony. No Black women attended the convention. None were invited." I would add that the document is closely patterned after the Declaration of Independence, which states "all men are created equal," a clause I would have thought signaled a red flag for the two women who wrote it. — J. Jackson women attended, and none were apparently invited. However, civil rights activist Frederick Douglass (1818 – 1895, born "Frederick Augustus Washington Bailey") was there, in fact the only African-American to attend the conference. Douglas had escaped from slavery in Maryland a decade earlier in 1838. It was he who encouraged women to include their right to vote in the convention's Declaration of Sentiments (*facing page*). From then on a suffrage movement grew, but, as with Native Americans struggling under their own oppression, both would have to wait until the 1920s for the right to vote to become law.

Frederick Douglass — American social reformer, abolitionist, orator, writer, and statesman.

Although "freed slaves" following the Civil War were accorded the right to vote with the ratification of the 15th Amendment in 1870, which stated neither the federal government nor the states could deny a citizen the right to vote based on their "race, color, or previous condition of servitude," it did not prohibit the denying of black women the right to vote, adding to an already racialist schism in the suffragist movement. Recalcitrant former slave-owning southern states then created new state constitutions, legislation, and regulations to block black (and poor white) voter registration — but not white males. The rise of the Ku Klux Klan and other white terrorist groups also used threats, violence, and murder to intimidate and obstruct blacks from voting. All of this led to a complicated protracted battle for the right to vote, culminating eventually in the 1965 Civil Rights Act to enforce the 15th Amendment.

Alice Stokes — American suffragist, feminist, and women's rights activist.

Moving into the present, it became clear that women, regardless of their race, were accorded 2nd Class citizen status by legal default. This became apparent, if doubted by anyone, by the failure of the states to ratify the Equal Rights Amendment (ERA) to the Constitution. The ERA was originally written in 1922 by two women, Alice Stokes Paul (1885 - 1977) and Crystal Catherine Eastman (1881 - 1928) and its intent was to guarantee equal rights to all Americans, regardless of one's sex — although "race" was omitted until Paul revised the amendment in 1943 to include the wording of the 15th Amendment. Numerous contentious splits within the

Crystal Eastman — American lawyer, antimilitarist, feminist, socialist, and journalist.

feminist movement plagued congressional passage of the ERA until 1972, when it finally garnered sufficient but tenuous support to be signed into law by President Richard Milhous Nixon (1913 - 1994) and then sent to the states, where it failed state ratification. That failure has continued to this day. It is largely due to women's concerns about gender roles — for example, military conscription, single-sex bathrooms, protective laws for alimony and social security (particularly for non-working women), the integration of men into women's colleges, and traditional mom-stay-at-home lifestyles. Such concerns resonated with the anti-feminist bias of many conservative women, particularly those holding "pro-life" values. So, legally — Constitutionally speaking — women remained locked out of the full "guarantees" set forth in the Bill of Rights 243 years ago.

Richard Nixon — 37th President of the United States.

Democratic Egalitarianism versus Capitalism, Communism, and Socialism

Platform holds that *Democratic Egalitarianism* is the only viable path to a humane society free of the tentacles of the New Feudalism. In the mid-1800s, there was growing dissatisfaction with capitalism and its concentration of wealth among the few and truly terrible conditions of poverty for working and "peasant" classes. European revolutionaries began to turn to *socialist* theories as a means of dealing with mass poverty. The central idea of socialism was to accord ownership of the means of production and goods to the government, specifically government controlled "collectives" of workers. This was closely related to the *communist* ideology of Karl Marx (1818 - 1883), which advocated for a system in which goods are owned in common by the people and are available to all as needed. By the late 1800s, "Marxists" began to formulate the foundations for a socialist rather than a communist revolution. However, this evolved further with the 1917 Russian revolution.

Karl Marx — German philosopher, economist, historian, sociologist, political theorist, journalist and socialist revolutionary.

In 1898, the Russian Social Democratic Labour Party was formed to unite various revolutionary organizations across the Russian Empire. In 1902, it split into several factions, including the Bolsheviks (Russian derived from *bolshinstvo*, "the majority") the Mensheviks (Russian for "the minority"), and the Mezhraiontsy ("Internationalists") who later joined the Bolsheviks. Following the 1905 Revolution's defeat at the hands of the Tsars (Russia's wealthy elite), further splits occurred, forming more factions. Under the leadership of Vladimir Lenin (1870 – 1924, born as "Vladimir Ilyich Ulyanov"), the Bolsheviks seized power from the Tsars during the October Revolution in 1917, and in 1918 changed their name to the All-Russian Communist Party. Lenin's administration redistributed land among the peasantry and nationalized banks and large-scale industry. They also withdrew Russian forces from World War I, and formed the Third Communist International in 1919 to promote world communism.[1]

Vladimir Lenin — Russian revolutionary, politician, and political theorist.

From 1917 to 1922 Lenin suppressed all anti-Bolshevik opposition, defeating both left and right-wing armies, and with his state security police, murdered or incarcerated tens of thousands in what became known as the Red Terror. Due to widespread famine, wartime devastation, and widespread protests and uprisings, Lenin encouraged the New Economic Policy — "a free market and capitalism, both subject to state control," while allowing the state socialist enterprises to operate at a profit. Lenin died in 1924, replaced by Joseph Stalin, unable to fulfill his socialist revolution. Lenin remains a controversial figure in history, hailed as a champion of socialism and the working classes, or condemned as the leader of an infamous authoritarian regime of political repression, murder and mass killings.

In other respects, however, *Platform* share's Lenin's critique of America's New Feudalism with which he was very familiar. Lenin believed that our representative democracy was only an illusion of democracy believing that our working middle class amounted to a "dictatorship of the bourgeoisie," meaning the islanding of wealth with the super-rich and the impoverishment of America's lower classes. Concerning our representative democratic system, he referred to it as a "spectacular and meaningless duel between two bourgeois parties," both answerable to "astute multimillionaires" (and now also billionaires) that exploited our

---

[1]Later participated in by Vietnamese revolutionaries, including Ho Chi Minh — a matter I take up in Objective #6.

working classes. Interestingly, he opposed liberalism, believing that it did not free workers from capitalist exploitation, perhaps anticipating the necessity of New Deal welfarism less than a decade after he died.

In 1991, the Union of Soviet Socialist Republics was dissolved. And with it went the socialist/communist visions of Lenin and other Russian leaders who followed him. Many independent countries resulted from the dissolution, including Russia or as it is called, the Russian Federation. The Russian Federation isn't made up of states like the U.S., but (currently) of 85 administrative entities, also called "subjects," with 8 Federal Districts which are composed of groups of subjects. The Federation is a multi-party representative democracy, with the federal government composed of three branches, not unlike out own: legislative, executive, and judicial. As of 2012, there were 48 registered political parties in Russia. The old communist party of the Soviet Union was abolished in 1991, but a new Communist Party was formed in the Russian Federation. It is a minor player today, however, dwarfed by the massive United Russia party formed in 2001. United Russia has no apparent common ideology, but is representative of whomever the president and other politicians they've elected to office, which reflects the regions from which they've come. One gets the feeling, Russia — still a super power — is trying to find its way in a complicated world.

§

The socialist-communist legacy of Lenin and later party leaders was one of oppression and violence, with scattered humanitarian successes. But the bad clearly imploded and took with it the good. Hitler's German Nationalist Socialism failed for its own shortcomings — racism, mass murder, and militarism run-amok. North Vietnam, North Korea, mainland China, Cuba, and other authoritarian socialist regimes have been no less ruthless in gaining and holding power, but they are still there, and like Lenin before he died, coupling socialist instruments with free-enterprise amid the suppression of democratic principles of egalitarianism. Most Americans have seen and heard enough of past and present models of socialism/communism to reject both out of hand.

But what of the hybrid socialist models hailed today as *democratic socialism?* These exist in some measure today in Scandinavia, and are known collectively as the "Nordic Model." Each have blended their former monarchies ("kings and queens") with parliamentary capitalism and socialist entitlement programs.

Whereas Marxist revolutionaries used socialism and tyranny to fabricate their oppressive societies, which failed, the Nordic Model uses purported social democracy as a way to transition from capitalism to democratic socialism, which has also failed. The Nordic ambition of ending capitalism caved to a gross welfare state of entitlements, capitalism, and parliamentary politics. In other words, more class society. We don't see the world rushing to them for what to do because the Nordics don't know what to do themselves. Especially since they opened the door to unrestrained international immigration that has plundered their entitlement programs and fomented resentment by its native nationalists. Currently, virtually all such models across Europe have lost favor and political "power." However, this is not to say that elements of the Nordic model do not have great value. In fact, *Platform* holds that they do and have integrated them into the Egalitarian objectives cited in this book. It is, further, much to the credit of the Scandinavians to explore this new political and economic territory with the highest intentions of doing good for their people. For this reason, *Platform* embraces the spirit of democratic socialism, if not its example, for humanitarian change than the demeaning welfarism foisted upon the American people by the New Feudalism.

Politics and Egalitarianism

Today, the U.S. remains firmly committed to its two party system of politics serving the special interests of what President Dwight David Eisenhower (1890 – 1969, born "David Dwight Eisenhower") called the *military-industrial complex*. It is a profiteering system that is directed and controlled by wealthy industrialists and those complicit with them in lower managerial positions, aided by their favored elected politicians in both the Republican and Democratic parties. Government workers are also complicit — if they want to keep their jobs. However, the expanding lower classes, the failing middle class, blue collar workers who've lost their jobs to automation and exporting of jobs to developing nations, disgruntled women, left leaning liberals, environmentalists, neo-socialists alienated from the Democratic Party, and others,

Dwight D. Eisenhower — 34th President of the United States.

wisely continue to look beyond it to a better way that does not favor impoverishment and human misery.

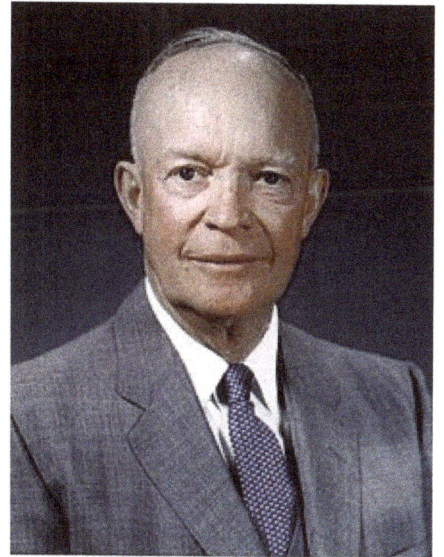

Platform, as a political vehicle for humane societal change, begins with an entirely different premise: true democratic egalitarianism cannot be harnessed to the shackles of capitalist, socialist, or communist ideologies in their current forms if it is to exist and prosper. Elements of each, however, seem both reasonable and inevitable. Nor can it proceed without the inclusion of women with equal rights, equal standing, and equal participation with men, and without regard to one's race. So remedied, *Platform* holds the promise for a genuine path to a humane and egalitarian society disinfected of poverty, sexism, militarism, *de facto* authoritarianism, racism and racialism — historically the key ingredients necessary to synthesize and sustain classism. Buy why is the inclusion of women so necessary?

One would think that the theory of egalitarianism is enough to answer this question. But, in fact, there is more to it. Women, when unfettered by the chauvinistic constraints of the New Feudalism, are from birth in possession of the principles inherent in egalitarianism: compassion, intellect, tolerance, forgiveness, clear thinking, moral and ethical bearing, strength of character, and acceptance of nature's diversity in our species. While these virtues are resident in some measure in many if not most men, they exist as latent shadows within the penumbra of machismo, militarism, intolerance, racialism, sexism, authoritarianism, and America's mass incarceration penal system — the key bearers to a violent class society expanding out of control. Without the centripetal balancing traits of female virtue institutionalized in society, men, given time, will as they always have, instinctively lead the human race by force, coercion, and chicanery into classism. This centrifugal force culminating in "male power and control" has dominated the world since the dawn of *Homo sapiens*. It is in their DNA and they cannot help themselves. Said another way, men need women as equals to be decent human beings.

§

Those seeking a political home in *Platform* are invited to study and embrace its principles and *Objectives* aimed at creating a genuine democratic egalitarian society. These Objectives are not presented in order of importance, as they are all equally important and work together as an integrated whole.

Democratic Egalitarian Objectives

OBJECTIVE #1
Healthcare — A Right, Not A Privilege

The presumption of free healthcare goes to the premise of a healthful society not dependent upon one's wealth to get whatever medical attention they need, versus the poor who get whatever politicians determine they shall have, including nothing at all. Humane, free, universal healthcare is typically rejected by the upper classes based on affordability. Who will pay for it? This is a smoke screen of the classist's mindset, which really means the poor don't deserve equal care — equal to what they have access to. You can't have equality in an egalitarian society, if it means denying equivalent healthcare to those who can't afford it.

The premise then that one person is deserved of superior health care to another based on wealth is, thus, core to the problem. Superiority complexes are rooted in class society. One's wealth equates to higher position and the privileges that go with it. The same egotist that believes this about themselves also believes that the poor are simply lazy and stupid, and, therefore, not worthy of the benefits of the wealthy classes. Success, it is presumed, equates to superior care. Indeed, one never sees the wealthy elite rubbing elbows with the poor in hospital waiting rooms, or under the bridge enjoying no benefits at all with the destitute poor who are homeless. Except in politically motivated photo shoots to garner votes.

But *Platform* suggests otherwise. Free access to healthcare is based on the principle of administering all vital essentials to its people without profiteering, including insurance policies. *Profiteering is the act or activity of making an unreasonable profit on the sale of essential goods especially during times of emergency.* The Veterans Administration's health care system, which I am familiar with from experience, in many respects provides a workable egalitarian model. Pharmaceuticals and procedures are not provided without evidence of efficacy. For example, a drug proven to be vital to patient health is opened for bid to the Pharma industry. The best formulation is then purchased at the lowest possible price, and it is the only option available to all patients in the VA system. Likewise, procedures deemed to be ineffective or less effective are either not offered or are replaced by those with a proven history of success or higher rates of success, even if the cost is greater. In both cases, taxpayers are supporting a better healthcare system for all, and the profit motive is reined in democratically so as to preclude profiteering.

Preventive medicine is essentially a void in the current for-profit healthcare system. This is because vitality threatens the profit motive based on pathology and drug profiteering. A healthful diet and regimented exercise are, thus, considered ancillary to healthcare. *Platform* holds that this relationship should be reversed: diet and exercise are taught and administered to in the long term at the front end of healthcare. As it is now, both are given nothing more than lip service in the healthcare industry — as though they are completely irrelevant! Healthcare, consequently equates to doctors offices, hospitals, and physical therapy. "Diet and exercise," mandatory and core to Platform's healthcare model, do not exist. People go to be treated, they do not go to learn about vitality. Of course, this favors pathology, treatments, profits, and patient debt, not vitality. The most effective way to reduce healthcare costs is to administer to vitality rather than "pathology for profits."

The VA Model currently serves only veterans, but through congressional reform, could be expanded nationwide for all American citizens, thereby by serving the egalitarian imperative of free and optimal healthcare, with an emphasis on preventive medicine through healthful diets and exercise, for all.

Objective #2
Government Employment Opportunities

In all cases, government jobs and pay should be based on education, experience, and time on the job; in other words, merit — not one's sex, gender bias, religious or atheistic beliefs, or race. To be clear, in an egalitarian society, women and men are accorded the same rights and opportunities. *Platform*, therefore, holds that half (50%) of all government jobs — municipal, county, state and federal — are divided equally between men and women based on merit.

Objective #3
Elected Officials

Because of anti-female bias and discrimination, women have been kept from their rightful representation in elected positions in government since the dawn of the nation! At the heart of this inequity is gender bias — specifically, that women are not naturally endowed with the intellect or emotional stability to run our country at the highest political levels. Consequently, this prejudice has kept their numbers to a fourth of men in both the Senate and the House. The same gender bias has influenced male and female voters alike to deny perfectly qualified women from becoming president and vice-president. This type of discriminatory behavior is based on sexist dogma with no factual basis. Once more, we are talking about the yoke of 2nd Class citizenship women are compelled to endure in a class society controlled by men since the inception of our country.

Because this defective perception of women is so deeply ingrained in American culture, *Platform* holds that all elected leaders should be rotated between the sexes at each election, including the presidency. For example, if a man is elected president in 2020, a woman must be elected in 2024. Likewise, a reelected president and vice-president team should alternate between women and men with each new term. For example, if in 2020 a woman is elected president, her vice-president must be a man; and, if their team wins the next election, the man becomes president and the woman serves as his vice president. *Platform* holds that the Constitution should be amended to provide for these male-female political rotations.

OBJECTIVE #4
The Popular Vote and Presidential Elections

The presidential election outcome is currently determined by the *electoral college*, not by the popular vote of the people. Which is to say it is "fixed" by the upper classes of the New Feudalism. This is blatantly clear if one reads the Constitution and the history of this bogus college's history. That the American people have put up with this corruption of democracy for so long is astonishing. Part of the problem is that few Americans can really explain what it is, why it exists, and who created it in the first place.

It is purported to be the only "fair way" to elect a president nationwide, giving states with smaller populations the same voter leverage as those with larger populations like California. But such logic is an intended foil created by the Old Feudalism to prevent a popular vote, one brought down to the present by the chicanery of our 2 Party political system of Democrats and Republicans who use it to keep control of political outcomes. Only when the popular vote loses to the electoral college's "elector votes," as it did in the 2016 election when Donald Trump won the electoral vote but not the popular vote, that the people begin to squawk about the illogicalness of the college, but then do nothing and forget about it.

So what is the electoral college?

The college is made up of Electors chosen from each state to elect the president and vice-president. Under Article II, Section 1 of the U.S. Constitution, each state chooses Electors in the same number that the state has senators and representatives. The Electors have the discretion to choose the candidate they vote for, and while in practice the Electors vote for the candidate that wins the most votes in their respective states, the Constitution does not legally mandate this of them. Right there everyone should be raising their brows with concern. In all the states except Maine, the candidate that wins a plurality of the popular votes wins all of the state's electoral votes. Generally, the parties either nominate slates of potential Electors at their state party conventions or they chose them by a vote of the party's central committee. But if the state Electors cannot agree amongst themselves on candidates, a complicated pathway of solutions leading right to the politicians in Congress can be laid. This process basically stands in the way of the American people, by popular vote, determining the outcome of the election. How did this happen?

The "Founding Fathers" decided that representatives of the people — not the people themselves — would elect the president by shadowy proxies. Alexander Hamilton explained their rationale, "A small number of persons, selected by their fellow-citizens from the general mass, will be most likely to possess the information and discernment requisite to such complicated [tasks]." Implying that the people are too stupid to think and decide for themselves. Apparently, enough of their "fellow citizens" — all white males — were dumbed down enough to go along with it. But as most of us know, we being the purported "general mass," it's not us casting the vote for our chosen elector. As stated above, its become party insiders or, with "back up" being their politicians already elected in Congress if rogue Electors get out of hand or can't come to an agreement amongst themselves. One could argue that the real problem is our 2 Party Political system, which controls the entire process.

Platform rejects the very premise of the Electoral College, and advocates its immediate abolition. Contrary to what the political elite of the New Feudalism want us to believe today, an informed American public is perfectly capable of choosing the president and vice-president themselves. The two parties may not like the outcome, but it would be a democratic outcome reflecting the majority of the American people, not a chosen few by proxy whom we've never met or heard of. The Constitutional roots of this mechanism of voter usurpation were mired in the disenfranchisement of women, American Indians, African Americans, and, let us not forget, the defense of human slavery and child labor. It is the legacy of white male supremacy of the Old Feudalism, and that is reason enough to abolish it once and for all. Seasoned politicians may vehemently disagree, but the Electoral College is just one of many barriers put in place by the Founding Fathers to preclude an enlightened and well-informed egalitarian society.

OBJECTIVE #5

Military Interventions and Declarations of Wars

Given the history of this country's militarism funneled through the "wars for profit" motive of the military-industrial complex, an informed people — who will carry the burden of the expense and casualties — should have superior decisional authority over any involvement leading to armed combat. What better way than a majority vote of the people? *Platform* holds that there are multiples ways (Objectives #5, #6, #16 and #22) to restrain these militaristic tendencies that inevitably lead to death and destruction. The most important way of all to achieve restraint is to present the facts of the matter before the people and their representative platforms. Then, as with presidential elections, let the people decide through a vote if a military solution is necessary or warranted. A substantial majority should approve of it (for example, 2/3 of the cast votes). Congress and the President can then take decisive and appropriate action according to the will of the people — not the military-industrial complex serving the upper echelons of the New Feudalism, who hunger for war profits and do not want the people interfering in their addiction. This is not to say that a strong and capable military force should not be in the ready at all times, only whether or not, to what extent, how, and exactly to what end it would be deployed should be up to the American people. Further, in time of war, industries serving the effort would not be funded by taxpayers on a "for profit" basis, as is the case now, thereby deterring the "war for profit" motive now preying upon the goodwill, trust, and naïveté of the American people.

OBJECTIVE #6

A New Cabinet Level Position: Department of Peace and Freedom

Platform contends that the President's cabinet is and always has been since George Washington (1732 - 1799),[1] out of balance because there is no contraposing voice espousing non-military solutions in the executive branch that is equivalent in stature to

---

[1]Washington was a core member of the Old Feudalism and no role model for egalitarian behavior. By 1799, slaves at his residence in Mount Vernon totaled 317, including 143 children. Scholars have determined that Washington controlled recalcitrant slaves, both male and female, through whippings and beatings, and also by the permanent separation from friends and family by sale. A firm believer in the inferiority of black African-Americans, he retained slaves before, during, and after his presidency. As Washington's plantation was operating at a loss, his wife freed their slaves a year after his death.

today's Secretary of Defense. To the same extent, the same opposing voice is necessary to counter today's Secretary of Homeland Security (militarized to defend the nations borders from illegal foreign intrusions) and the Secretary of State (least militarized as the federal government's official minister of foreign affairs). Thus, by seating a powerful voice at cabinet level to advocate for peaceful rather than military or CIA (Central Intelligence Agency) clandestine solutions, one more significant step towards egalitarianism is taken.

The suggestion that seeking peaceful rather than military solutions to international threats to the country signals "weakness" to our ostensive adversaries is the classic argument of the elitist of the New Feudalism as it has been in the distant past. But weakness is a smokescreen and terror term to scare Americans into war, when the applicable term should be "war profiteering." It is nothing less than an industrialist's

George Washington — 1st President of the United States.

addiction for more money and political power. But it is not the lives of the industrialists that are on the line. It is the lives of young men and women, typically still too intellectually immature to know better. Two glaring examples (among others) of this stand before current generations to reflect upon because both cost tens of thousands of American lives for nothing but war profits, and at least several million of our "framed" adversaries who were, in fact, bullied by our industrialists and elected politicians of both political parties into armed resistance. These are the Vietnam War and our current Middle East military interventions.

The War in Vietnam

The first example of military adventurism for profits was against the Vietnamese people. Characterized by U.S. politicians as rabid "commies out to get us" under the contrived "domino theory of communism," nothing could be further from the truth. A truth my post-WWII generation was never taught in school.

The Vietnamese had been brutally "ruled" by French colonialists since the 1800s. Vietnamese revolutionaries later wrote in words to the effect, "the blood of the Vietnamese people fed the rubber tree plantations of the French colonialists." Plantations that gave us Americans, the French and others tires (and other things made from rubber) that we used on our automobiles, trucks, and tractors.

Ho Chi Minh — Vietnamese revolutionary and politician.

Having had enough of this, Vietnamese dissidents traveled to France in the early 1900s, including later revolutionary icon Ho Chi Minh (1890–1969, born "Nguyn Sinh Cung"), to petition the French government and later the allied powers at the 1919 Paris Peace Conference (Versailles Peace Conference) following World War I. This effort was to obtain recognition of the civil rights of the Vietnamese people, end French colonial rule in Vietnam, and ensure the formation of an independent government of the Vietnamese people. President Woodrow Wilson (1856–1924) represented the U.S. at the Conference, but like other representatives of the allied powers present, refused to hear the Vietnamese. Had Wilson listened and supported their cause for independence, many historians and antiwar advocates like myself, believe the entire Vietnam debacle never would have happened. But I am not surprised their words fell on deaf ears, as it is well-known today that Wilson was an avid segregationist during his Presidency and his racialist views would have readily transposed to the Vietnamese as inferior puppets of the French and deserved of no civil rights, let alone independence from colonial rule.

Woodrow Wilson — 28th President of the United States.

Lacking support from the western powers, and already leaning towards socialist principles as a way to help their people, Ho and other Vietnamese dissidents turned to the communist revolution — the Russian Bolsheviks under Lenin — for training in revolutionary principles and methods, and later arms support in what would be a successful effort to drive the French from their homeland in another 34 years. Ho also used this training to serve as an advisor to the developing armed forces of the Chinese Communist insurgents led by his contemporary in arms, Mao Zedong (1893 – 1976), who, like Ho, was preparing militarily for Chinese independence from western rule by proxy. Later, Mao aided Ho's forces in the Viet Nam war.

Mao Zedong — Chairman of the Communist Party of China.

With the arrival of World War II, Ho's revolutionaries, now armed in the tens of thousands, ironically aided the U.S. in their mutual effort to drive the Japanese (now at war with the U.S.) out of Indochina, including French colonial Vietnam. The precursor to the CIA, the OSS (Office of Strategic Services), now working closely with Ho's forces, agreed to bring Ho's request for support for independence before President Harry S. Truman (1884–1972). But like Wilson, Truman chose to ignore Ho. Ho's coalition for liberation, called the Viet Minh, then turned their military attentions against the French, called the "First Indochina War," driving them out of Vietnam following their defining victory at the Battle of Dien Bien Phu in 1954. This was followed by the involvement of the United States and others (via the Geneva Accords that eventually divided the country in half, north and south) to negotiate a new arrangement among the Viet Minh, the French, and anti-communist Vietnamese factions within Vietnam. All of which failed eventually, leading to the Second Indochina War, known by Americans today as the Vietnam War.

Harry S. Truman — 33rd President of the United States.

Rather than let the Vietnamese people decide for themselves their future, the U.S. decided to meddle and then engage full blown militarily to oppose the Viet Minh forces coming south from "North Vietnam," and the National Liberation Front operating out of Laos, known by Americans as the Viet Cong. This escalation by the Americans occurred under the presidential administrations of Eisenhower, Kennedy, Johnson, Richard Nixon (who eventually ended U.S. military involvement), and, at its very end, Gerald Ford (who ordered final evacuation of all U.S. personnel). As in WWII and the Korean War (and the continuing U.S. occupation there), American industrialists and politicians assumed pro-war stances in Vietnam that generated profiteering that caused U.S. taxpayers billions of dollars and 65,000 American dead and hundreds of thousands more wounded. A lost cause from the beginning, because facilitating Vietnamese independence was always the right thing to do. Eventually, the American people came to their senses and pressured their government to end the war. A war from which they never psychologically recovered from to this day. To many Americans, Vietnam remains the greatest military blunder in the history of the United States, but to American industrialists and their investors it was further proof that "war for profits" suited the upper echelons of the New Feudalism just fine.

Middle East Wars ("War On Terrorism")

U.S. military interventions in the Middle East were sealed for the future when what would become British Petroleum began exploiting petroleum (crude oil) in Persia (today: Iran) in 1908. In the aftermath of World War 1, Great Britain had seized much of the Middle East formerly held by the Ottoman Turks, and following their expulsion, the British, with the help of France and the tacit support of the Allies, began politically divvying up the region into new states to suit their own purposes. Syria, for example, became a French protectorate based on an earlier League of Nations mandate. The coastal areas (settled largely by Christians) were split off to become Lebanon — another French protectorate. Iraq and Palestine became British mandated territories. Iraq became the "Kingdom of Iraq," and now included large populations of Kurds, Assyrians and Turkmens, many of whom had been promised independent states of their own. Most of the Arabian peninsula became the Kingdom of Saudi Arabia in 1932. All of this eventually inured to religious and political instability in the area.

The (British) Palestine Mandate was then split in half. The eastern half of Palestine became the "Emirate of Transjordan," eventually becoming the Kingdom of Jordan, or simply Jordan as most Americans know it today. The western half of Palestine was placed under direct British administration. At this same time, the British Balfour Declaration of 1917 promised regional Jews an independent state in Palestine. Since the 1800s Jewish Zionists had already targeted Palestine as their "promised land" based on their interpretations of ancient history and had encouraged Jewish migration into the area long before WWI. The Jewish population of Palestine numbered less than 8 percent in 1918, but Jews were now given free rein by the British to immigrate, and also establish the foundations for a Jewish state under the protection of the British Army. A Palestinian revolt against this migration was suppressed by the British in 1936.

The Holocaust then contributed to an increased migration of Jews into the area following WWII. Muslim Palestinians living in the Palestine Mandate observed this "invasion" of Jews, as they perceived it, into what they had thought was to be their legal homeland based on their own communications with the British and allies during WWII. But it was now clear to the Palestinians that any such promises were tantamount to a betrayal by the British and French, and, further, that the Balfour promise of a Jewish state was now eminent. Soon acts of terrorism against the British to force their hand one way or the other were carried out by both Jewish terrorists and Palestinian resistance groups. Following the failure of the British to create partitioned Jewish and Palestinian states in the same area, the British appeased the Jews and sanctioned the Israeli state in 1948. They then pulled out of the area. As quickly, war between the new state of Israel and the Palestinians and their Muslim allies across the Middle East followed.

Amid all of this, it was just a matter of time before U.S. corporations jumped in to exploit the "black gold" needed to support its burgeoning automobile industry that depended on gasoline. Eventually shrewd Arab leaders formed OPEC to consolidate their own hold on oil profits, and American interests became entangled with theirs. Complicating the situation further was widespread resentment of Israel by Muslims across the Middle East and elsewhere, including Afghanistan — the historical bridge leading to China and the Far East. Since the end of WWII, America's support of Israel and the need to protect its own oil interests in the Middle East, put the U.S., alongside Israel, at the top of the enemies list of the Palestine Liberation Organization (PLO), Al-Qaeda, Hezbollah (based in Lebanon and a proxy for Iran), Hamas (occupying the Gaza Strip), ISIS, the Taliban (Afghanistan), and many other militant Islamic groups that want the end of the Israeli state and American forces out of the Middle East.

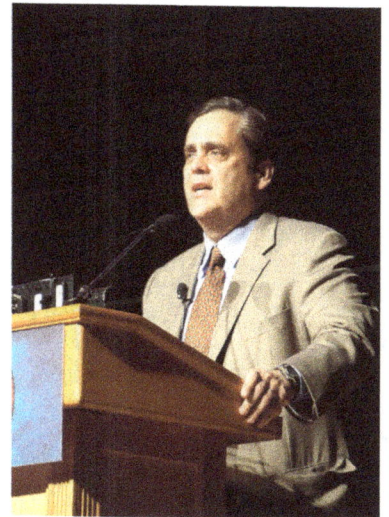

Jonathan Turley — American lawyer, legal scholar, writer, commentator, and legal analyst in broadcast and print journalism.

As a result, the U.S. military entrenched itself deeply in the expanding Middle East crisis, including Afghanistan, in the longest protracted war — the "War On Terror" as it is known by Americans today — in our country's history. A war that reached our own shores in numerous terror attacks costing thousands of American lives on "9/11." But what did this really mean to the military-industrial complex? U.S. taxpayers have spent not billions, but trillions of dollars in this ongoing war at home and abroad. Jonathan Turley (born, 1961), the Shapiro Professor of Public Interest Law at George Washington University, has written about this during President Barack Obama's presidency:

> In January 1961, US President Dwight D. Eisenhower used his farewell address to warn the nation of what he viewed as one of its greatest threats: the military-industrial complex composed of military

contractors and lobbyists perpetuating war.

Eisenhower warned that "an immense military establishment and a large arms industry" had emerged as a hidden force in US politics and that Americans "must not fail to comprehend its grave implications." The speech may have been Eisenhower's most courageous and prophetic moment. Fifty years and some later, Americans find themselves in what seems like perpetual war. No sooner do we draw down on operations in Iraq than leaders demand an intervention in Libya or Syria or Iran. While perpetual war constitutes perpetual losses for families, and ever expanding budgets, it also represents perpetual profits for a new and larger complex of business and government interests.

It's no accident. The same "complex of business and government interests" learned from the war in Vietnam that it could simply play the same card in the "war on terror" across the Middle East. One would think that we learned that the North Vietnamese armies and Viet Cong guerillas never had any such interest in coming to attack us, because they never did. Their only interest was for us to leave and let the Vietnamese people decide their own fate. Today, American tourists, including former combat soldiers who served in that war, are welcome to come visit the country. In fact, the new Socialist Republic of Vietnam that emerged from the war recently invited President Donald Trump to visit, which he did, and for whom the people extended a warm welcome that stunned the world. Trump did what former presidents Wilson and Truman refused to do, which would have spared us a completely unnecessary war — by simply acknowledging the right of the Vietnamese people to determine their own future.

But the brains behind war profiteering, as President Eisenhower warned, suited post-WWII politicians the likes of Wilson and Truman just fine to brutally savage the lives and landscape (we recall the devastation of Agent Orange on the native flora of Vietnam) of the Vietnamese people for money and power, certainly not honor. And now in the wake of Vietnam, we find a new generation of politicians and war profiteers pointing not at "socialist commies" to fear, but "terrorists." But who are these terrorists and how do they correlate to war profiteering? Turley again:

The new military-industrial complex is fuelled by a conveniently ambiguous and unseen enemy: the terrorist. Former President George

W. Bush and his aides insisted on calling counter-terrorism efforts a "war." This concerted effort by leaders like former Vice President Richard Bruce Cheney (born, 1961) — himself the former CEO of defense-contractor Halliburton — was not some empty rhetorical exercise. Not only would a war maximize the inherent powers of the president, but it would maximize the budgets for military and homeland agencies.

This new coalition of companies, agencies, and lobbyists dwarfs the system known by Eisenhower when he warned Americans to "guard against the acquisition of unwarranted influence... by the military-industrial complex." Ironically, it has seen some of its best days under President Barack Obama who has radically expanded drone attacks and claimed that he alone determines what a war is for the purposes of consulting Congress.

Dick Cheney — 46th Vice President of the United States.

The core of this expanding complex is an axis of influence of corporations, lobbyists, and agencies that have created a massive, self-sustaining terror-based industry.

If one understands the underlying profit motive in Vietnam, then it does not require a degree in rocket science to understand the rationale for bringing the American military-industrial complex to the Middle East. *Platform* holds that America's industrial intrusion into the lives of Middle Easterners to exploit their natural resource — crude oil — was simply a stepping stone to a more profitable military intrusion. To pull this off, American interventionists had to invent a new enemy: "the terrorist." Terrorists would be anyone who refused to accept the rearranging of Middle Eastern territories, all engineered by America and its Western allies between WWI and WWII as explained above. The rise of "terrorist" groups, as our politicians now call them, out to get us is no accident, but the terrorists do not see themselves as such. Like the Viet Minh and the Viet Cong, they see themselves as freedom fighters who do not want America and its allies telling them what to do or to accept their foreign military occupations.

However, complicating matters for the terrorists are their ancient religious rivalries, readily exploited by the military-industrial complex and politicians as being anti-democratic. Throw into the mix Russian and Communist China's own

interests along with the threat of nuclear war, one gets the picture that things are getting totally out of control. Worse yet for these terrorists, if one can imagine, was the creation of the democratic Jewish State of Israel in the heartland of the Palestinian people. But history shows that this heartland was once the heartland of the Jews predating the arrival of Jesus (himself born a Jew) and Christianity, and also the Muslim faith brought by Mohammed less than a thousand years ago. Before all three of these major religions were born, they all shared the same came ancestry written in the Old Testament. But the fact is the Arab state coalitions cannot honestly accept an independent Jewish state being forced upon them, particularly the displaced Palestinians stuck in the Gaza Strip. Unfortunately, the anti-Israel Arab coalition battle-cry is currently "Palestine from the Jordan River to the sea," and some calling simultaneously for the extermination of the Israeli state, the Israeli Jews, and all Jews everywhere. That, of course, is Nazi Jew extermination talk. Which isn't going to go over well with Jews anywhere and one hopes with non-Jews either. Platform opposes any kind of extermination rhetoric or actions coming from any side, and respects Israel's right to defend itself as do Jews anywhere. Logically, if Palestinians really want peace with Israel and its supporters than it needs to end its own death cult rhetoric and practices and terminate its relationships with Arab Jew hating states and their proxy terrorist groups calling for the same. There's an important history lesson here worth bringing up.

Gerald Ford – 38th President of the United States.

Denazification of Germany, dismantling of fascism in Italy, and termination of imperial Japan's militarized monarchy, and the evil likes of all their collaborators, were not optional following WWII. It was compulsory under allied military occupation. Allied military bases still have presence in those countries nearly 80 years later as a consequence of the mass destruction those countries brought upon the world. The solution was replacing totalitarian with democratic institutions. Clearly, the Palestinians should avoid further bloodshed and destruction and follow suit by joining the rest of the peace loving world. So that they don't feel singled out, American Indian nations faced the same thing but had to learn the hard way to get with the program. Many fought and died to defend what they thought was theirs, others saw the light and realized that superior military forces always win and submitted to civilization and the white man's laws. True freedom always comes at a price.

OBJECTIVE #7

Free Enterprise and Democratic Socialism: Serving An Egalitarian Society

Platform holds that the islanding of extreme wealth derived by any means favoring the upper classes (millionaire-billionaire-trillionaire) in the New Feudalism, and that results in an expanding class of the impoverished and destitute, is inconsistent with an egalitarian society. *Platform* holds further that a mandatory investment of a substantial percentage of such extreme wealth in America's infrastructure for the benefit of all — to be specifically determined by the popular vote of the people — is consistent with egalitarianism.

Platform holds that this reinvestment of wealth is best instituted within a new amalgamation of America's free-enterprise system of capitalism, democratic socialist instruments for the humane dispersion of wealth, and a reformed U.S. Constitution that accords equal rights to men and women, all based on egalitarian principles. Democratic egalitarianism is neither profiteering, anti-profit, fascist, socialist, communistic, nor militaristic — all of which have failed people through the ages because all have inured to a pathological acceptance of institutionalized poverty, war and classism.

OBJECTIVE #8

Egalitarian Platforms vs. Two Party Politics

Platform holds that our *de facto* "two party" system of Democrats and Republicans is unquestionably controlled by the wealthy elite of our country and serves the interests of the vast majority of Americans *only as they see things should be* through the lens of their military-industrial complex. This collusion of Democrats, Republicans, and the wealthy classes can be traced to their historical roots in the Old Feudalism. It comes as no surprise that the Constitution is "silent" on the issue of political parties.

The "Founding Fathers" initially took a dim view of political parties, fearing that such "factions" would undermine the stability of the nation at the time they authored the U.S. Constitution. Thus, fearing the popular vote of the American people, they created the Electoral College (discussed earlier) in 1787 to prevent the peoples' interference in presidential elections. In his essay, Federalist #10, Alexander Hamilton (1757 - 1804) saw any given faction of the American people as a

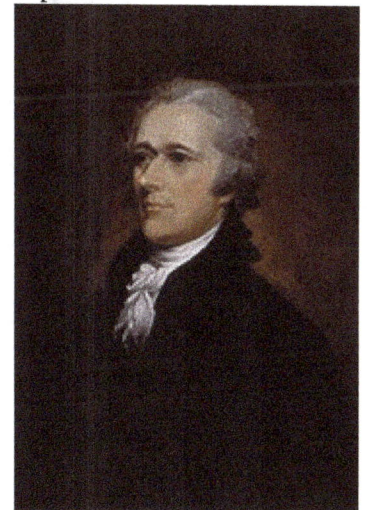

Alexander Hamilton — American statesman, politician, legal scholar, military commander, lawyer, banker and economist.

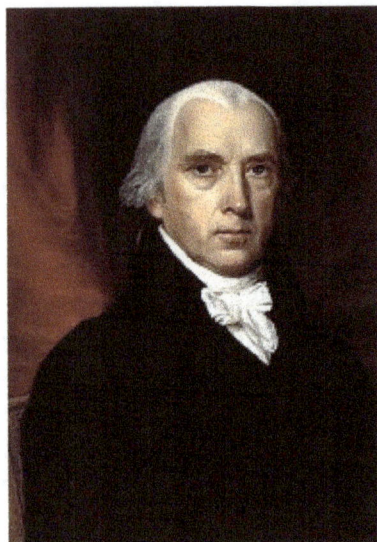

James Madison — 4th President of the United States.

potential "overbearing majority" that would degrade elections into "factions" of "mischief."[1] A faction, he defined as "a number of citizens whether amounting to a majority or minority of the whole, who are united and actuated by some common impulse of passion, or of interest, adverse to the rights of other citizens, or to the permanent and aggregate interests of the community." Political rival James Madison Jr. (1751 - 1836)[2] also concurred in his own paper, Federalist #9. And so, George Washington, who also opposed a party system as being inherently divisive, and belonging to no political party himself, was elected president in 1789.

Ironically, it was during Washington's administration (1789–1799) that Hamilton and Madison reversed course and came around to the understanding that having strong political parties supporting candidates of their choice, and who would represent the special interests of their wealthy benefactors, would give their men the best chance of winning the presidency — and, for that matter, right on down the line from appointments in the judiciary, to the members of Congress. Two parties immediately evolved, ironically during Washington's administration!

These were the conservative (and basically anti-slavery) *Federalist Party* spearheaded by Hamilton — President Washington's Secretary of the Treasury — which favored a powerful federal government, a centralized banking system, manufacturing, strong economic growth, and getting back on good terms with Great Britain. All the "makings" for the Old Feudalism. Opposing the Federalists was the *Democratic-Republicans Party* — also known as the *Republican Party* — founded by Madison and Thomas Jefferson (1743 - 1826), Washington's Secretary of State.[3]

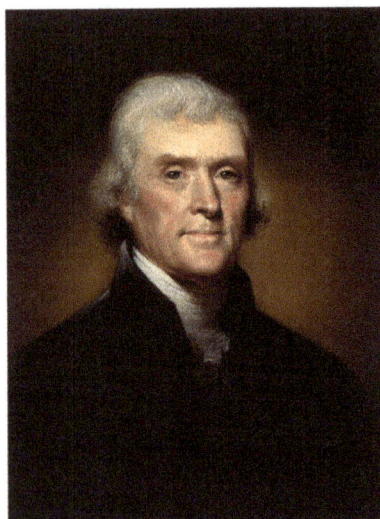

Thomas Jefferson — 3rd President of the United States. 1st United States Secretary of State.

[1]Hamilton, thought to have owned several slaves in his younger days, was by the time of the American Revolution, and outspoken abolitionist.
[2]Madison believed in slavery, owning more than 100 slaves on his plantation.
[3]Jefferson, like Madison, also believed in slavery, owning more than 600 slaves on his plantation with a majority having been born there. Evidence suggests that whippings and beatings were rare, but imposed by Jefferson's overseer — under Jefferson's orders — when necessary to stop fights, stealing, and other disturbances. There is a consensus among modern scholars that Jefferson had a clandestine sexual affair with one of *his*

(Continued on page 49)

But Washington himself opposed this development through the two terms of his presidency and on into private life, saying at his Farewell Address (September, 1796), "I have already intimated to you the danger of parties in the state, with particular reference to the founding of them on geographical discriminations. Let me now take a more comprehensive view, and warn you in the most solemn manner against the baneful effects of the spirit of party, generally."

With Washington's retirement and return to his plantation at Mount Vernon (located in Virginia near present day Alexandria), the Federalists won the 1796 election with their candidate John Adams (1735 – 1826),[1] defeating Jefferson's Democratic-Republican party. But infighting and divisions among the Federalists soon began, with Hamilton now opposing the policies of Adams, such that Jefferson and his followers then took the 1800 election. The Democratic-Republican party then held power through to the 1824

John Adams — 2nd President of the United States.

elections. At this time, both the Federalist and Democratic-Republican parties dissolved. The latter reformed into two new parties, the National Republican Party and the Democratic Party, each absorbing adherents of the Federalists into their ranks. The Republicans held sway briefly during John Adam's son's (John Quincy Adams) presidency, before dissolving in 1834 to form the WHIG Party. The Democrats held office until 1861, except for two one term presidencies taken by the WHIG Party (1841-1845 and 1849-1853). The WHIG Party then

[1]Adams, one of the very few presidents who did not own slaves before the Civil War, vehemently opposed slavery, saying so in an 1812 letter to Robert J. Evans on June 8th, 1819, "I have, through my whole life, held the practice of slavery in such abhorrence, that I have never owned a negro or any other slave, though I have lived for many years in times, when the practice was not disgraceful, when the best men in my vicinity thought it not inconsistent with their character, and when it has cost me thousands of dollars for the labor and subsistence of free men, which I might have saved by the purchase of negroes at times when they were very cheap."

(Continued from page 48)
slaves, Sally Heming, who, ironically, was also a half sister to his late wife [same white father (a Heming), but different mothers, Sally's mother being a slave to Heming]. This affair began 7 years after Jefferson's wife died. During 2017 archeological excavations at Monticello, Sally Heming's slave quarters was discovered adjacent to Jefferson's bedroom. Their sexual relationship apparently began in France in 1789, when she was 16, and he was 46, Jefferson having been a U.S. envoy to France before the French Revolution in 1791. Sally, her brother, Jefferson's young daughter with his late wife, and others were brought along for formal educations in France. When they all returned home together (1789), Sally was pregnant. It is my opinion from gleaning much of the source material about this, they were a couple clearly in love, having had six children together, all of whom lived in the house at Monticello with their mother and father. Their relationship lasted for 37 years, ending with his death in 1826. A 1998 DNA study confirmed a direct link between the descendents of Jefferson and Sally's children and Jefferson, ending 170 years of controversy and speculation.

Abraham Lincoln — 16th President
of the United States.

dissolved in 1854, replaced by a new Republican Party formed in 1854. Abraham Lincoln (1809 – 1865) won the election of 1861, returning the presidency to the (re-born) Republican Party, when the nation then entered the Civil War.

Although the new Democratic and Republican Parties that had emerged by the time of the Civil War (*facing page*) are the direct descendants of the parties of the same namesakes today, they differed markedly. The Democratic Party then was very much pro-slavery, individual rights and state sovereignty, opposing any anti-slavery measures. They naturally carried the Southern plantation states and those newly forming states that provided for slavery after the 1820 Missouri Compromise was repealed in 1854 with the passage of the Kansas-Nebraska Act — which provided for the expansion of slavery into some new U.S. territories as discussed earlier. This pitted them against the repentant anti-slavery Republican Party that now favored banks, railroads, and other economic policies of the WHIG Party. Polarization and violence over states rights and the expansion of slavery in the new territory, coincided with Lincoln's semi-anti-slavery presidency, and the nation then erupted in the Civil War (1861-1865). But what we were never really taught in school is that, arguably, it is this war, in particular, that truly gave birth to America's military-industrial complex. Even politicians in the day, some of those just discussed, knew and even lamented the fact:

> Worse than traitors in arms are the men, pretending loyalty to the flag, who feast and fatten on the misfortunes of the nation, while patriot blood is crimsoning the plains of the south, and bodies of their countrymen are moldering in the dust. - U.S. House Committee on Government Contracts, March 1863

From that costly — but profitable! — war to the present has seen a welcome shift in the political landscape of the two parties. Slavery is no longer an issue! But that's about it. Today, as in 1861, both parties are together entrenched in seamless servitude to the military-industrial complex. Both crave political power equally as though it were heroin, a necessary addiction if they are to feed the agendas of the super-rich. But both are also impotent to halt the spiraling and expanding lower classes, because their political landscape renders it impossible. The

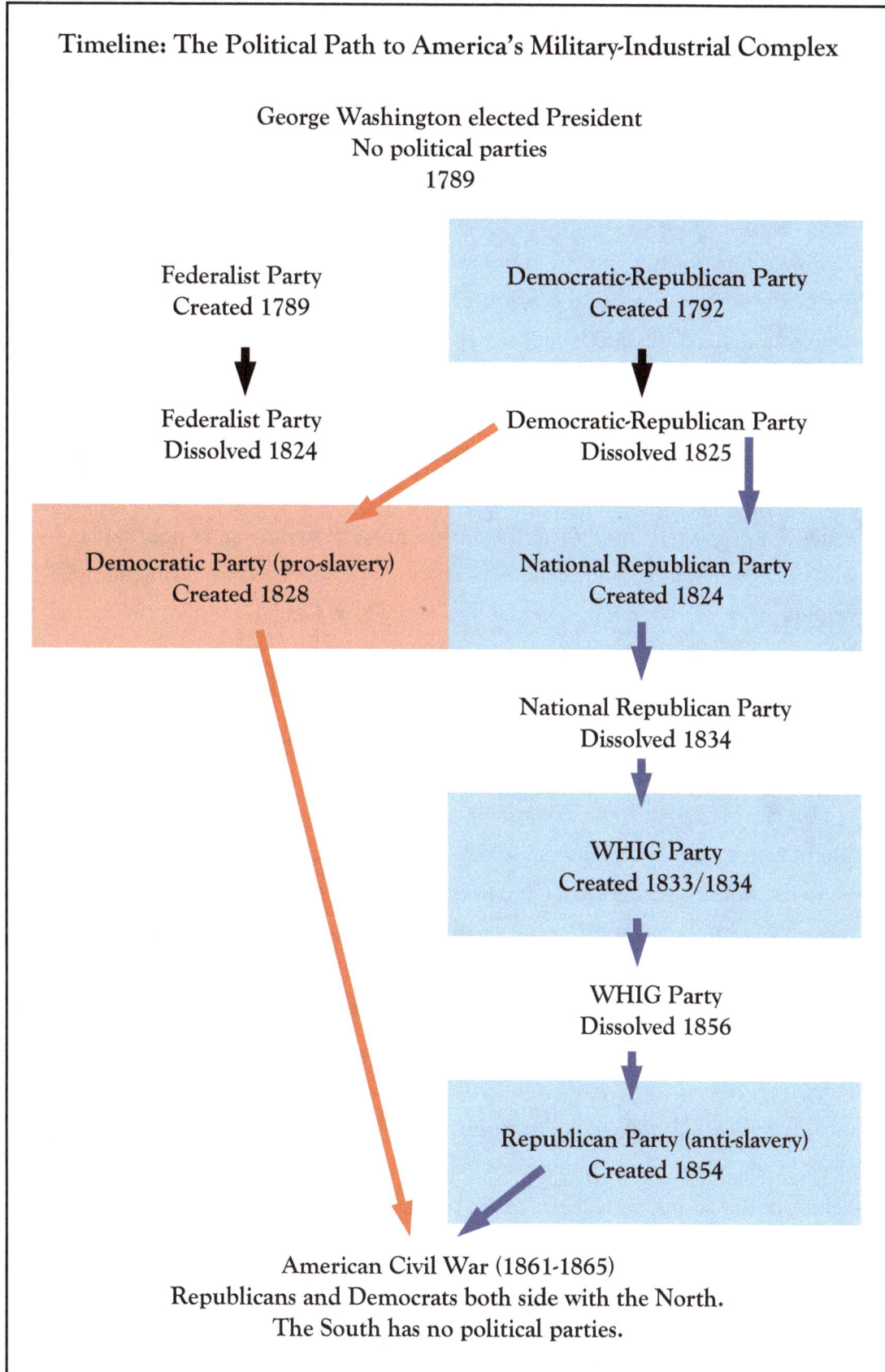

Timeline: The Political Path to America's Military-Industrial Complex

George Washington elected President
No political parties
1789

Federalist Party
Created 1789

Democratic-Republican Party
Created 1792

Federalist Party
Dissolved 1824

Democratic-Republican Party
Dissolved 1825

Democratic Party (pro-slavery)
Created 1828

National Republican Party
Created 1824

National Republican Party
Dissolved 1834

WHIG Party
Created 1833/1834

WHIG Party
Dissolved 1856

Republican Party (anti-slavery)
Created 1854

American Civil War (1861-1865)
Republicans and Democrats both side with the North.
The South has no political parties.

islanding of wealth in the New Feudalism at the top is a political corollary of impoverishment of those at the bottom. There is no expatiation for the poor, except at the bottom. The shrewd super-rich, shaking their heads in disgust, look down in every respect from their perches atop high-rise corporate headquarters, castle-like mansions atop mountains, and private jets zooming by overhead where legroom is never an issue. The lower classes they see beneath them are evidence of their own superiority measured in terms of their military and industrial might, personal wealth, and political power over others. The lower classes are unrehabilitatable and, therefore, disposable, an aggravating menace of lost souls, each deserved of their fate. This is the undisguised face of the New Feudalism, and it is completely out of control. *Platform* contends that the only way to loosen their iron grip is to facilitate a diverse spectrum of political platforms whose egalitarian principles, Objectives, and candidates are both inseparable and meaningful to the American people who need them the most — not a steady stream of politicians who can't say enough about themselves and their personal accomplishments and whose parties, like themselves, are facades of the New Feudalism that bring nothing but more misery to the poor.

OBJECTIVE #9
Abolish America's Mass Incarceration System

Platform holds that America's system of incarceration and punishment is inconsistent with a humane, egalitarian society. The U.S. incarceration rate is the highest in the world — greater than China's or Russia's! It is a rate that has rapidly increased since the Vietnam War (see chart, *facing page*). *Platform* contends that criminal behavior by Americans today (and in the past) is a perfectly natural response to the exploitations of its people in the New Feudalism (and its progenitor, the Old Feudalism). While there are many antisocial behaviors contributing to crime and incarceration, poverty underlies most. It is a fact that desperate people, including the poor, will engage in criminal behavior as a means to their very survival. Examples are drug dealing, prostitution, illegal gambling (including dog fights), online scams, petty theft, armed robbery, and even murder.

Not surprisingly, the military-industrial complex that is fueling classism in the New Feudalism, perceives and exploits poverty and crime as significant conduits to profiteering through mass incarceration. Those most destitute are the most vul-

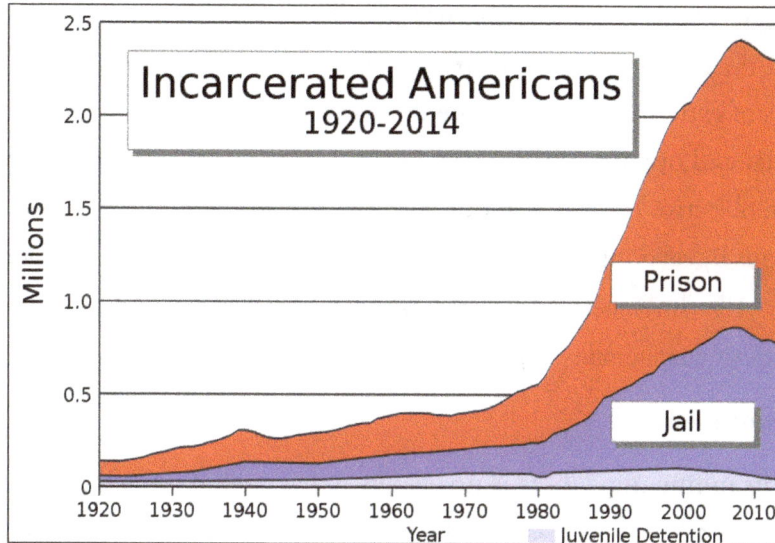

Incarcerated Americans
1920-2014

nerable because they cannot afford bail or the same legal council as the wealthy, and, thus, they linger on in the system longer than others. Which is to say that a growing population of poor criminals inures to greater islanding of wealth in the upper classes. This is done through privatization of prisons as well as by government run prisons and jails.

Today, taxpayers foot an annual 81 billion dollar burden to house over 2 million incarcerated Americans! But in addition to those numbers are another 5 million living on probation or parole, incurring an additional 100 billion dollars to cover court costs, probation services, and other fees paid by offenders. According to the U.S. Bureau of Justice Statistics, that puts 1 in 38 persons in the United States living under correctional supervision — not including another 54,000 living in juvenile detention. In sum, 181 billion dollars are lost to crime every year. But even this does not include the costs associated with building more and more prisons that will add more yet to the tax burden.

Platform holds that the same funds channeled away from correction supervision and to the poor in keeping with egalitarian principles could lift hundreds of thousands permanently out of poverty, and millions more as the poverty factor shackled to incarceration abates. If it weren't that the New Feudalism has weaponized poverty to take from the poor and destitute (via the taxpayer) through an attrition of what few defenses they have to protect themselves with, to give to the military-industrial complex. A *national disgrace*. So, this has to change, but the math favors a way out.

Because America's "crime and punishment syndrome" is so pervasive and entrenched in the New Feudalism, *Platform* holds that the only remedy is to redirect the excesses of extreme wealth into the democratic socialist instruments that can provide relief and opportunities to the defenseless and destitute of the lower classes. The objective is to abolish our current criminal detention system of mass incarcerations by severing its roots in poverty. With that abolition also goes three of the most evil crimes associated with mass incarceration: *capital punishment, life sentences without the possibility of parole,* and *solitary confinement.*

Capital punishment

Besides its inhumanity, there is no evidence that capital punishment ("death penalty") deters crime, which is why the majority of nations in the world today have abolished it. Those who argue in favor of it cite justifiable *retribution,* particularly for the most heinous of crimes, such as those committed by serial killers, religious terrorists, child rapists, and other psychopaths. But there is evidence that these offenders are themselves victims of genetic corruption (e.g., schizophrenia), severe abuse (e.g., child rape), prescribed psychotropic medications causing aberrant and dangerous behaviors for which there is no accountability from drug manufacturers and physicians — and also the FDA (Federal Drug Administration) and the bogged-down and effete 2011 Food Safety Modernization Act. Common sense should signal to retributionists that no person of a sane mind would willingly choose psychopathy as a lifestyle. Yet, state laws suggests they do, and accordingly have provided for the death penalty to punish them. But state sanctioned murder, for that is what it is, only debases humanity's moral compass further in favor of violence built upon more violence.

Life sentences without the possibility of parole

Life without parole is simply an extended death sentence, and, therefore, a segue to retaliatory punishment by retributionists.

Solitary confinement

Solitary confinement (isolation of a prisoner from other prisoners) is an inhumane but inevitable consequence of American prison life. It is used in various ways. For example, to punish or constrain a dangerous or recalcitrant prisoner who cannot control their violent or other problematic behaviors that puts other inmates or prison personnel at risk of harm and even death. It may also be used to protect prisoners who are either dangerous to themselves, or who are at risk of being harmed by other prisoners. Whatever the reason for isolating the person, it is going to be harmful to that person's mental stability because our human species did not evolve through natural selection to live alone in claustrophobic solitude apart from others, including nature itself. Thus, solitary confinement is nothing more than another layer of psychological violence perpetrated by our retributive penal system of mass incarceration serving the military-industrial complex.

OBJECTIVE #10
Free Daily Meals

Platform holds that hunger in America, like other plights of the poor, is effectively institutionalized by the humiliating and deficient social welfare programs of the New Feudalism. The widespread distribution of "food stamps" (now replaced by a debit type bank card), for example, reflects the desperation of the lower classes who have insufficient means to provide enough food for themselves. *A national disgrace.* That food banks in nearly every city are ubiquitous points directly at the failure of the food stamp program and the failed architecture of the U.S. Department of Health and Human Services that deploys its "food credits" to the poor. The fact that the military-industrial complex exports food abroad, that supermarket shelves are full, and that eateries of every kind are flourishing almost everywhere, is incontrovertible evidence that there is more than enough food and that hunger is simply a disgraceful and inevitable symptom of the New Feudalism's classism. Arguably, hunger, like crime, has been weaponized against the poor by the military-industrial complex. People who are hungry and malnourished cannot be expected to behave in any other way than desperate. Desperate people can be expected to engage in criminal behavior to survive. Thence to jails and prison.

Platform holds that in the land of plenty, Americans should not have to beg for food. But they must as the system is set up to humiliate and punish the poor as retribution for not being able to pay for their food. This awareness and experience seemingly lies beyond the grasp of the wealthiest classes of the New Feudalism. But on closer analysis, it is purposefully intended. Social workers at the doling end are instructed by upper bureaucratic management to wrangle and "penny pinch" those in need, taking away with the slightest suggestion that the poor have earned the smallest amount of income that other necessities readily consume. All of this "food terrorism" is orchestrated by our politicians, Democrats and Republicans alike, decreeing that anything more than the very least is unacceptable to the military-industrial complex that controls the New Feudalism from above. Ironically, and sadly so, most of this intimidation is conducted in the field by social workers who are women: women behaving like controlling men who are further up the government's chain of command who determine what they will and will not do. The cliché often heard by women living in poverty whom I've interviewed, "Women are the worst enemies of other women in our society," clearly satisfies the sexist mentality of our male-dominated political system that creates these weaponized programs that pit lower level female bureaucrats and social workers against destitute women in need. *Another national disgrace.*

As a universal safeguard against hunger and America's "food stamp tyranny," *Platform* holds that a government administered "free food" cafeteria style system be orchestrated nationwide, serving healthful meals daily to anyone who enters the premises at no cost. Whether the diner be a billionaire or penniless, all are welcome with no questions asked and no "registration" is required. Nor are donations or tips to cafeteria workers allowed, as these are forms of distinguishing the "haves from the have-nots," replacing one form of humiliation to the have-nots by another. Funding is the responsibility of the federal and state governments — funds derived democratically from the coffers of the military-industrial complex.

OBJECTIVE #11
Home Ownership: A Right, Not A Privilege

Platform points to the fact that housing is a growing crisis among the lower classes due to the disparity of wealth in the New Feudalism. As discussed earlier, after WWII what were affordable homes were turned into commodities for real estate speculation. As housing prices escalated to facilitate the "upward mobility" scheme exploited by the middle class, joined in by real estate agents, banks and other lenders and speculators, a snowball effect arose that left fewer and fewer behind who would be able to afford anything. Recent data for the super rich worldwide is revealing of their stake in all of this. According to one research paper, they account for over "U.S. $5 trillion, or 3% of the world's real estate holdings. This is a huge proportion considering this population is only 0.003% of the world's population."[1] This does not include the New Fuedalism's iron grip on our public lands.

[1]Savills and Wealth-X (2014). *Around the World in Dollars and Cents* (PDF). p. 2.]

Left completely out were the burgeoning lower classes, including remnants of the middle working class. This set the stage, also as explained earlier, for unprecedented levels of slum lording, particularly in the inner cities where industrialists once housed their factories and provided jobs. But as those jobs were exported abroad to exploit impoverished nationals who would take just about anything offered, unemployment in America was the result, leading to new levels of poverty, homelessness, and crime. Those without inheritances, without higher education, without jobs or were just making it with minimum wage jobs, along with the elderly poor, drug addicts, disabled veterans surviving Vietnam and Middle East militarism, convicted felons, and the mentally challenged, were the first victims to fall into the lap of the entitlement programs or the ranks of the homeless. For this enormous and expanding underclass today, there is seemingly no way out of it in the New Feudalism.

Platform holds that the right solution is to make home ownership a Constitutional right and not a privilege of those with wealth. The national disgrace of transforming "homes into houses" — tradable commodities for profits sake — has devastated large numbers of Americans and their families, who have no way into a home of their own. Since such an idea has no quarter of acceptance within the ranks of investors, banks, speculators, and most Americans who own homes and pay mortgages, the transformation from renting and homelessness due to poverty to home owning will be the responsibility of a politically transformed government based on the guiding principles of egalitarianism. Such a transformation will not be led by the upper classes, but by an informed people who need it the most and by those of a caring and compassionate nature.

A looming question much bandied about is whether or not affordable housing will ever be possible again? *Platform* holds that this is possible through a protracted process within the context of other egalitarian reforms specified in the Objectives of this book. That process principally follows along two lines of reform aimed at ending housing as a mechanism for upward mobility: *abolishing landlordism* (an extension of feudal serfdom discussed below) and *abolishing profiteering at the point of sales for all citizens, including the poor.*

Abolish landlordism

Landlording harkens back to medieval feudalism, the progenitor of institutionalized classism that the lower classes still suffer from today in the U.S. It is also a

variant form of the highly exploitative sharecropping system freed-slaves and poor
whites engaged in the aftermath of the Civil War (*facing page*). In any case, the
owner of the land (e.g., the landlord) lets the tenant use the land (e.g., live in their
house or apartment owned by the landlord) for a fee. Landlords try to get the most
they can (profiteering) based on the local economy. Because such landlording is
typically predatory, many communities have imposed rent control ordinances to
protect the poor. Among the poor living in impoverished neighborhoods, or even
in middle class or upper middle class neighborhoods, landlording typically trans-
poses to Section 8 tenancy. Landlords cunningly purchase cheap homes, as many as
they can afford, and enter into contracts with the government to receive payments
from both the tenant and government, if possible, far in excess of any mortgage
they may have entered into to purchase the house. Such arrangements also enable
landlords to hold properties in abeyance for years until property values have so in-
flated that they can sell out at a substantial profit. Such properties are now even further beyond the reach of the poor. Again this is a variant of the upward mobility
mechanism used by most Americans if they can pull it off.

As fewer and fewer Americans are able to qualify to purchase anything, they either rent from landlords if they can get qualified on their own, or enter into Section 8 contracts if they can show proof of low income (e.g., Social Security disabil-
ity) and openings are available. But as it is, an enormous and growing demand today for Section 8 and other types of public assistance housing far outweighs the
availability of rentals, forcing many to sleep in their cars if they have one or descend
into the ranks of the homeless in the streets. This shortage of rentals enables landlords and slumlords to raise their rates even higher, burdening the taxpayers who
fund Section 8 and public assistance housing. In some communities, elevating
rental costs is a way to exclude the poor, replacing them with tenants who can afford to pay higher rent. In this respect, both skyrocketing housing prices and high
rents have been "weaponized" against the poor — all in the name of profiteering.

Platform holds that the only way to stop this exploitation is to rein in and eventually abolish landlordism as an instrument of profiteering. Such rentals should be
severed from landlords and then sold to the poor based on Basic Income discussed
(**Objective #13**) and lending rights discussed earlier. Situated in their own home,
the poor can take stock of their lives in security and stability, and with mandated
counsellorships (**Objective #13**) take advantage of opportunities for personal
growth to become productive members of society. The abolition of all Section 8

(*Left*) 1862 photograph of the slave quarter at Smiths Plantation in Port Royal, South Carolina. (*Right*) After the Civil War (1865), slaves turned to sharecropping to survive, as this family is doing 76 years later in Greene County, Georgia (1941). After World War II, mechanized farming brought an end to share cropping.

and other public assistance housing (**Objective #14**) will, with these egalitarian measures, eventually end all predatory landlordism and real estate speculation based on profiteering.

The question of landlord severance is then raised: how shall this occur? There would be no severance if the owner intended to retain rental properties for their own use (e.g., family members). But that would depend on the number of rental units that are involved. If the landlord owned, as an example, 1,000 rental homes as the person did that I alluded to earlier in this book, what the reduction would look like and at what rate would be a matter of public debate and Congressional legislation. It would also depend on the type of rental property. Apartments, for example, would be purchased by the government at point of sale prices (see below) and sold to the poor in the form of collective ownership, one of the humane instruments of social egalitarianism attributable to Communist principles. Another possibility: a group of millionaires propose to purchase ten run-down apartment complexes in a neighborhood devastated by poverty, restore them to handsome units that would please any eye, provide security, and donate them for individual or collective ownership under the government's auspices or partnership, and at point of sale reduction costs. This would set several things in motion: create employment to restore the properties, provide for home ownership, and return their initial investments that could then be redeployed in other areas to the same end. Perhaps others might wish to join in the effort too, thus expanding and strengthening the coalition's economic base through additional funding or even property donations. Again, the purpose of property severance is to broaden the diverse landscape of affordable home ownership for all, and deter feudal instruments of landlordism and profiteering.

Abolish profiteering at the point of sale

The ever-escalating price of homes in the U.S. is alarming. This reflects the attitude and practice of home buying Americans — to purchase a home at the lowest price possible, with the understanding that if one is going to resell it for whatever reason, one hopes to sell it at a maximum profit and not a loss. Of course, this is a reflection of human greed directly attributable to classism. In fact, this attitude is also taken to the extreme level of enterprise by real estate speculators — the arch enemies of home owning for home ownership's sake. Their singular purpose is to make money either by reselling or renting the property, or both, whichever path is more profitable in the short or long term. This clash with egalitarian principles, which now favors the upper classes of the New Feudalism, would seem irreversible — and will be if those suffering at the hands of it do nothing about it. This is where "free enterprise" has gone astray, and that an egalitarian society must rein in.

Platform suggests that all points of sale be reduced by either a fixed percentage or a percentage rate based on a sliding scale relative to the selling price. For example, if one purchases a home for $100,000 dollars, it cannot be resold for more than the buyer's original point of sale reduction percentage. In this way, speculation is prevented, new speculators are deterred from threat of prosecution, and essential home ownership will gradually prevail at lower and lower price thresholds. At the same time, speculators who bought low at poverty stricken rates (for example in predatory foreclosures), will not be able to sell out and inflate the selling price due to the same original point of sale reduction percentage. In summary, Americans will be compelled to abandon self-serving feudalist impulses that transpose to the poverty and misery of others. But in doing so, the emergence of affordable housing for all will result in a better society.

The question may be raised, do these reforms preclude one from owning more than one home at any cost to create? Absolutely not! If personal success in one's business pursuits enables it, then why would government interfere? New feudalist landlordism and real estate speculation schemes based on profiteering are the issues, not personal home ownership, which under the new egalitarian laws will prevent rising real estate prices.

OBJECTIVE #12

Education: A Right by Merit, Not A Privilege by Wealth

Platform holds that all primary and secondary education in public schools should, as it is now, be free to students and paid for by federal and state governments. Advanced degrees in the arts and sciences, however, should also be free to students at state colleges and universities, but entrance is contingent on academic merit — not family wealth. Technical schools (for example, for training automotive mechanics and electricians) should also be free to students, but are also based on merit. Private schools, colleges, and universities may also participate and receive government funding at the same rates provided to state colleges and universities, but they must also provide free education to their students. All current student debt should be extinguished by an act of Congress.

The issue of some schools being superior to others may be raised, with the concern being that students attending schools in impoverished communities where crime rates are higher will be at a disadvantage when applying to higher institutions of education where "merit" is a deciding factor. Of course, this is exactly the situation now in the New Feudalism. But we are no longer talking about feudalism in our new democratic egalitarian society are we? So, while such a concern is understandable, it is misplaced.

OBJECTIVE #13

Basic Income: A Right, Not A Privilege

Platform holds that there should be a Constitutionally guaranteed personal income for all its adult citizens. That income should not be conducive to poverty and be fully in concert with other Egalitarian Objectives detailed in this book.

There is no current "welfare income" that can sustain one at or above the poverty line. For example, Social Security income is not a sustainable income without other supportive income or entitlements in today's New Feudalism. It is a distinct "welfare" program to help keep poor and disabled Americans from falling through the cracks and into the ranks of the homeless. But even with Social Security, people still fall through the cracks because it isn't a sustainable income and destitute people may not know how to obtain other government assistance or may not even qualify. Without a basic sustainable income, the poor remain trapped and destitute in the lower classes and in homelessness.

The political right, libertarians, and the upper classes of the New Feudalism generally all target welfare programs like Social Security as the bedrock of "losers" and the road to Socialism that will destroy America's free-enterprise capitalist system. But such criticism is entirely self-serving, as the military-industrial complex they themselves defend and thrive on exploits the taxpayers far more so to fund its militarism abroad and at home. Just as it exploits cheap labor abroad and leaves the American labor force in shambles, ruthlessly exploits and destroys the earth's natural resources, and islands its profits in the upper classes of the New Feudalism. If this is what the vocal advocates of free enterprise have in store for the world, victims of the New Feudalism will naturally resist and choose from necessity any instrument of socialism or communism to survive and to avoid homelessness. What do they expect people to do in the absence of a just social, political, and economic system of egalitarianism?

Libertarians, interestingly, have long railed against both Democrats and Republicans as being shades of the same quasi-Capitalist-Socialist welfare system they despise. Laurence M. Vance, a Libertarian with whose views *Platform* shares very little in common most of the time, has written an assault on Republicans in the current Trump Administration with which *Platform* does concur:

Laurence M. Vance, Ph. D. — Director of the Francis Wayland Institute, Adjunct Instructor in Accounting at Pensacola Junior College, and an Adjunct Scholar at the Ludwig von Mises Institute. He holds degrees in history, theology, accounting, and economics.

After many years of Democratic control of both houses of Congress, Republicans captured the Senate during the presidency of the Republican Ronald Reagan and held on to control of it for six years. They did absolutely nothing to stop the onslaught of socialism. In fact, they raised the Social Security and Medicare tax rates to bolster those socialist programs. If only we had control of the House, said the Republicans. During the last six years of the presidency of the Democrat Bill Clinton, Republicans had a majority in both houses of Congress. They did absolutely nothing to stop the onslaught of socialism. In fact, they increased the refundable Earned Income Tax Credit (EITC) every year to redistribute even more of the incomes of

American taxpayers. If only we had a Republican president, said the Republicans. When the Republicans finally got their Republican president in George W. Bush they had a perfect opportunity to abolish the federal government's socialist programs and restore the United States to a free and capitalist society. The Republicans controlled both houses of Congress for more than four years during the Bush presidency. They had not had absolute control of the government since the first two years of Republican Dwight Eisenhower's presidency. Again, they did absolutely nothing to stop the onslaught of socialism. In fact, they expanded Medicare, created the TSA, and tremendously increased the budget of the Department of Education. The Republicans had another chance to roll back socialism when they controlled both houses of Congress during the first two years of Trump's presidency. But again, they did absolutely nothing to stop the onslaught of socialism. In fact, they could not even come together to repeal Obamacare, even though they had railed against it since the day the Democrats passed it in 2010.

> The conclusion is inescapable: Republicans are powerless against socialism because — as shown by their words and deeds — they are socialists themselves.

The edict, "powerless against socialism," is what *Platform* agrees with. What are people to embrace when the New Feudalism of free enterprise expects the lower classes to live on crumbs and under bridges with no genuine economic opportunities to lift themselves up from poverty? Socialism provides retaliatory economic instruments for the expanding lower classes. *Platform* suggests that these instruments should be delivered through Democratic Egalitarianism, not through traditional Socialist models that have also inured to classism — and as Vance correctly points out, more welfarism.

Platform holds that a Basic Income for all — from the forthcoming trillionaire class to the penniless — is a key pillar of Democratic Egalitarianism and freedom from a humiliating, degrading, and wasteful welfare state that inures to classism and more poverty. In this interpretation, a robust free enterprise system with embedded socialist instruments will march together hand and hand to create the new egalitarian society. Analysts will determine at which income above the Basic Income taxation will occur and at what percentages. With Americans then standing together on their own feet, it may be that one day the Basic Income will no longer be needed, but will be there *just in case*.

Mandated counseling

The impoverished middle and lower classes will need more than a Basic Income to facilitate their ascent from the bowels of the New Feudalism. They will need dedicated counselors to help them reorganize their lives into a state of stability, from money management to job opportunities to healthcare and exercise responsibilities to new home ownership — and also security against predators who would take advantage of them. Those rising from homelessness and mass incarceration will need additional professional assistance. This will also be a critical transition period that may require both close monitoring and protection by law enforcement, particularly where there has been a history of family violence.

OBJECTIVE #14
Abolish Government Welfare "Entitlement" Programs

Platform holds that all government welfare programs are antithetical to egalitarianism by definition and should be abolished. Such programs are the brainchild of the New Feudalism, dating back to President Franklin Roosevelt's New Deal in the 1930s. These were the desperate seeds of Socialism planted by the New Feudalism to stave off a people's Marxist type revolution during the country's Great Depression. The Communist Party was active in the U.S. then (and still), and many Americans were lured to its promise of an equitable redistribution of the country's wealth. But being a decent people, Americans were aghast at the inhumane excesses and violence of the Bolshevik's Communist Revolution (and later, Joseph Stalin's Great Purge of 1936-1938) and forever rejected totalitarian systems of Socialism and Communism in favor of democracy and hard work.

So Americans stood in bread lines as needed and toiled in the Works Progress Administration (WPA) of the New Deal. The WPA, the government's first major socialist program, provided jobs and income to the unemployed (mostly men) during the Great Depression to help stabilize and improve the country's infrastructure. This included such projects as building bridges, roads, and parks, many of which are still in existence and used today nearly a century later. Elements of the New Feudalism, however, saw in this "dependent work force" a means to an end:

the threat of a return to joblessness *or* servitude in the new burgeoning military-industrial complex. Japanese imperialist expansion in the Far East and German Nazis expansion in Europe during the 1930s, set the stage for American militarism in the 1940s.

WWII, following on the heels of WWI (which cost taxpayers 32 billion dollars), replaced the failing New Deal economy, and was the great door opener to mega-war profiteering, costing taxpayers 60 billion dollars! This is what President Eisenhower was warning the American people about. But both of those wars paled in costs compared to today's budget in the Afghanistan and Iraq military interventions, a whopping 2.4 trillion dollars by 2017!

The new worker class of the military-industrial complex, however, was never intended by the industrialists to become wealthy itself. They were to do the work, and understand in the clearest terms that troublemakers were expendable. In the end, due to unions and expanding government regulations, the decision was made to replace them all with off-shore factories where desperate foreign nationals would work for virtually nothing and under conditions — "sweat shops" — that Americans themselves wouldn't stand for. But this is the nature of the New Feudalism, and Americans in the lower classes are coming around in their own ways to seeing it for what it is. Nevertheless, countless Americans continue to hang on to their minimum wage jobs, entitlements if they can get them, and promise for a better life suggested in our Declaration of Independence — *Life, Liberty and the pursuit of Happiness* — for which many have unwittingly given their lives in our country's wars for profit.

The upper classes are watching all this with earned consternation and trepidation, and their politicians — now divided amongst themselves as to what to do about it — are furtively trying to deal with the near impossible. The political right has fired a volley across the bow of those Socialist leaning Democrats warning America of its impending Marxist tyranny if they follow in that direction. The political left returns fire promising more entitlements to protect the people from the political right that will take it all away and leave them with nothing. The world watches, as it always has, to see what the Americans will do. *Platform* holds that they will choose egalitarianism over either, as both are simply quasi-socialist-capitalist instruments of the New Feudalism.

Objective #15
Prisons and Jails Are No Place for Women

Platform holds that most criminal and anti-social behaviors committed by women leading to incarceration can be traced to poverty and/or any of the following influences:

- The unbearable and negative influences of controlling men.
- Physical and mental abuse, coercion, and violence perpetrated by men upon women.
- Personal betrayal and abandonment (including children) by men.
- Institutions, legal and illegal alike, controlled by men that prey upon and discriminate against women.
- Law enforcement dominated and controlled by sexist men (only 12% in law enforcement are women) who are prejudiced against women and purposefully discriminate against them (for example, blame women for being raped, fail to process rape kits, and exploit them for sexual favors if arrested).
- A legal system that discriminates against women because it is dominated by sexist men and created by sexist men.
- A political system and government that is manifestly populated with and controlled by men (for example, only 23% of women are U.S. Representatives; 25% in the U.S. Senate).
- Economic (e.g., wages), sex and gender, and racial discrimination due to the ratification failure of the Equal Rights Amendment to the U.S. Constitution.

Because of the above, *Platform* holds that with the exception of confirmed criminal psychopathy requiring mandatory medical/psychiatric intervention and humane detention monitored by female advocates for women's rights, women should not be committed to jail or prison for any reason.

At first thought, the suggestion that women not be incarcerated in our penal system makes no sense or may even evoke outrage. But both responses stem from the *male chauvinism syndrome* that is inculcated in Americans from birth, women and men alike, by the ubiquitous military-industrial complex. Meaning, women deserve to be punished because they are inferior to men and because of their intrusions into traditional male territories. Even biblical teachings blame women for corrupting men and the world at large. It comes as no surprise, as an example, that this syndrome leads men — and women who are brainwashed to think and behave like men in the military-industrial complex — to blame women for being raped by men. In some countries it is taken to the extreme of executing women for "causing" men to rape them.

For this reason, *Platform* holds that this syndrome creates a blind eye in society that willfully ignores sexist causality so that it may incarcerate women for crimes that are committed against them by men, brainwashed women, and their institutions. This is particularly difficult for many — but not all — men to understand or to show contrition for in the face of, in spite of the historic and extant cultural evidence right beneath their noses. Evolving from a lesser paradigm of negative chauvinistic value to a higher one of enlightenment and willful change, is apparently a bridge too far for those too infected by the syndrome. Thus, *Platform* suggests that it is best extinguished by righting an obvious wrong and immediately removing all women from America's deplorable and sexist system of mass incarceration.

OBJECTIVE #16
Equal Rights Amendment
Equality Or More Kudos for the Military Industrial Complex?

Platform holds that passage of the Equal Rights Amendment is, in spirit, the right thing to do, but would it be just another mechanism — in the absence of a galaxy of egalitarian reforms — for compelling male gender roles in women in the New Feudalism? There is some evidence for this concern based on recent behaviors and policies of women serving in the military-industrial complex. An example (*page 68*): U.S. Army Reservists Sabrina D. Harman, Lynndie England, Megan M. Ambuhl and six men were all convicted in court-martial in connection with the Abu Ghraib torture and prisoner abuse incidents between 2003 and 2004. The prison's commanding officer, Brigadier General Janis Karpinski — blaming orders from above to skirt accountability — was demoted in rank and relieved of her command, but not court-martialed and convicted.

Another example, according to UNICEF (United Nations Children's Fund), over a ten year period in the aftermath of the U.S. Gulf War in 1991, five hundred thousand (500,000) Iraqi children died as a result of U.S. bombing raids and sanctions imposed on Iraq. American Secretary of State Madeleine Albright (born, 1937, as "Marie Jana Korbelová" in Prague, Czechoslovakia), a Democrat at the time serving under President Bill Clinton (born, 1946), when asked on American television whether the

Madeleine Albright — 64th United States Secretary of State.

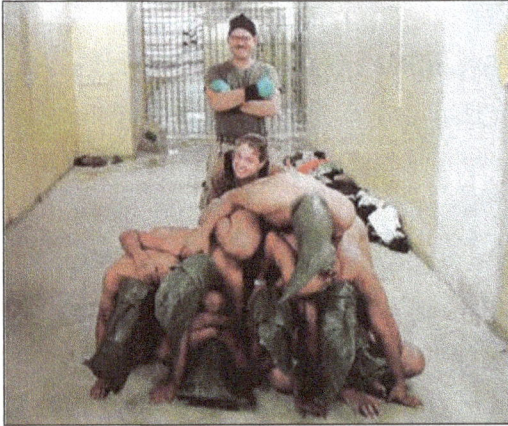

Sabrina Harman poses for a photo behind naked Iraqi detainees forced to form a human pyramid, while Charles Graner watches.

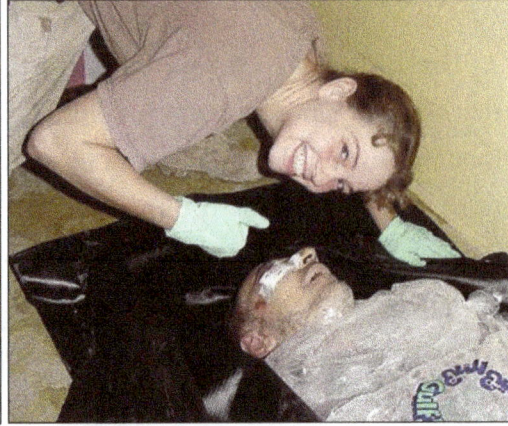

Sabrina Harman posing over the body of Manadel al-Jamadi, an Iraqi prisoner who was tortured to death in United States custody during interrogation at Abu Ghraib prison in November 2003.

Lynndie England pointing to a naked prisoner being forced to masturbate in front of her. England being escorted out of Williams Judicial Center at Fort Hood after being sentenced to three years in prison.

Ambuhl (left) observing as Lynndie England pulls a detainee known as "Gus" from his cell by a leash.

Brigadier General Janis Karpinski, commanding officer at the prison, was demoted to colonel on May 5, 2005.

deaths of more than 500,000 children was a price worth paying, answered: "We think the price is worth it." But Albright has also been accused of such callousness in other venues caught on film, spreading ethnic hatred towards Serbian victims of the Kosovo War in 1999. More recently, Albright was a public supporter of candidate Hillary Clinton during her 2016 presidential campaign. At a Clinton campaign rally in New Hampshire, Albright said, "There's a special place in hell for women who don't help each other." But, in fact, it was a sexist slight aimed at younger women who supported Clinton's forthcoming primary rival, Senator Bernie Sanders. Albright attempted to walk it back in a New York times op-ed not long after, "I absolutely believe what I said, that women should help one another, but this was the wrong context and the wrong time to use that line. I did not mean to argue that women should support a particular candidate based solely on gender." But her credibility, as well as hush-mouthed Clinton's, was stained and lost upon Sander's dedicated flank of the Democratic Party to this day.

All of this is not intended to slight women, for what has gone awry above is but a fraction of similar male transgressions in the larger stream. This is simply to say that both women and men are vulnerable to these kinds of depraved, violent, and run-amok male gender roles inculcated by the military-industrial complex.

OBJECTIVE #17

A Green Society: Federal Mandates for Free Enterprise and Democratic Egalitarianism

Platform holds that government and private industry, under congressional mandates, should cooperate to facilitate and create a "green infrastructure" ranging from food production, energy, transportation, education, employment, and housing. And those participating businesses should be rewarded with significant tax incentives. Further, in keeping with the spirit of egalitarianism, those businesses demonstrating an equality of the sexes from "ownership to the work force" would receive preferential consideration over those that do not. Examples:

Solar (sun) and Wind Power. This technology is rapidly advancing worldwide as replacement technologies for the fossil fuel industry.

Electric cars. According to the U.S. Department of Energy, compared with internal combustion engine cars, electric cars are quieter, have no tailpipe emissions, and lower emissions in general. This technology is also rapidly advancing and truly represents the future. *Platform* holds that ownership of electric cars should be a constitutional right, not a privilege of the wealthy classes.

A national network of high-speed trains using electricity as the motive power. High speed rail is rapidly advancing internationally, while the U.S. remains stagnant and trapped in Amtrak's 19th century fossil fuel polluting technology, with no alternative but to use airlines that are contributing significantly to global warming. Electric trains now travel at speeds up to 200 mph, and some faster yet. They are sleek, modern, comfortable, and do not pollute the atmosphere.

Federally subsidized local Organic Farms, Ranches, and Community Gardens. This program would be connected to **Objective #23**. The entire people and animal food chains are contaminated by old and new generations of toxic herbicides, pesticides, and petroleum based emissions from heavy equipment.

An important path away from this dilemma is to government subsidize sustainable and localized organic food and animal feed production, including humane care of animals used for consumption. At the same time rolling back large scale corporate and private operations that depend on "cost-effective contaminants" that pollute food, feeds, and the environment, and that contribute to the inhumane treatment of animals by using "mass incarceration" confinement systems. These are all based on mass marketing principles and international markets that translate to profiteering at the highest levels of the New Feudalism, and which disfavor and impoverish working classes that make their profits possible.

Organic farming is on the rise across the U.S., but is still infitismal compared to large scale agribusiness, which itself is largely subsidized. According to downsizinggovernment.org, "Farm programs are welfare for the well-to-do, and they induce overproduction, inflate land prices, and harm the environment. They should be repealed, and farmers should support themselves in the marketplace." And here is where organic farming comes in precisely, as they are currently smaller family operations. Take the state of Iowa, for example — according Karen Perry Stillerman, a senior communication strategist and senior analyst in the Food & Environment Program at Union of Concerned Scientists:

> Iowa is plagued by a heavy presence of multi-national agribusiness
> and a conservative state Farm Bureau, which do not, unfortunately,

favor out of the box thinking for what types of agriculture would be best for Iowa families and Iowa family farmers.

With corn prices as low as they are currently, and many farmers feeling the heavy burden of commodity conventional agriculture at the moment, Iowa farmers, Iowa state government and Iowa State University would benefit by studying their neighbor's vibrant local organic food system. Wisconsin's family farmers have benefited by investing in more organic acreage, and now is the time for Iowa to pass policies that encourage Iowa farmers to transition to organic.

Green food and feed production can move across state and even international boundaries — but not based on profiteering. Objective #23 targets 18-20 year olds to help work and run these operations, providing them with technical and educational skills, the ability to help feed themselves and their communities, restore and protect local environments, and learn to get along with others in keeping with egalitarian principles. Community student exchange programs would be encouraged to expose students to America's diverse ethnic populations, thereby breaking down barriers based on racialism and classism.

OBJECTIVE #18
Homelessness: Eliminate, Not Criminalize

Platform holds that today's homelessness is a crisis created by the New Feudalism. There is a distinct trend emerging to criminalize homelessness as a way to deal with it. Incarceration of the homeless feeds the coincidental "prisons for profit" motive of the military-industrial complex. *Platform* holds that *criminalizing homelessness is a national disgrace.* Homelessness can be solved through egalitarian interventions. Due to its complexity — there are many reasons why individuals become homeless — no single type of intervention will work for all. Advocates for the homeless know exactly what interventions are needed.

This is especially true of convicted felons who cannot find jobs, those who are disabled, and those who are drug addicts. Homeless camps I have visited are characterized by a bizarre cohesive social order that does not factor according to contemporary theories of normal human socialization. I will say this, the depths of human desperation and depravity can breed unrequited behaviors that from one person communicating fragmented logic, confusion, tolerance or indifference in one

Vagrancy is the condition of homelessness without regular employment or income. Vagrants usually live in poverty and support themselves by begging, garbage scraping, petty theft, temporary work, or welfare (where available).

moment will illicit equally fragmented responses of confusion, predation, violence or genuine fraternity from another in the next without rhyme nor reason. Paranoia dwells deep in many. The de-evolution of human behavior occurring in the shadows of the New Feudalism is more than a national disgrace, it is an alarming and chilling nightmare of human degradation. Further, amid this backdrop of human depravity come reports of proliferating communicable and contagious diseases.

Studies show a humanitarian societal streak running through the classes above the homeless, but ends with the suggestion of contiguous communities with the homeless. Most Americans simply don't know what to do with the homeless, but feel a responsibility to help them. *Platform* holds that the homeless must be removed from their street lives of pathological vagrancy to address their individual needs and be spared forthcoming criminalization laws that will very likely make them long term or permanent members of America's mass incarceration penal system. The process must require a humane and monitored system of triage to place them where their individual needs can be addressed (*facing page*). Prisons and jails should not be their destinations. Homing them indiscriminately in communities,

Triage for Homeless Individuals and Families		
Classification	**Intervention**	**Resolution**
Single female	Interview	Her own home*
Single male	Interview	His own home*
Male living in car	Interview	His own home*
Female living in car	Interview	Her own home*
Couple or Family living in car	Interview	Their own home*
Single female or male with children	Interview	Their own home*
Mother + Father with Children	Interview	Their own home*
Male with mental disorder	Diagnosis	Treatment facility (men)***
Female with mental disorder	Diagnosis	Treatment facility (women)***
Male drug addict	Diagnosis	Treatment facility (men)**
Female drug addict	Diagnosis	Treatment facility (women)**
Male felon	Interview	Supervised half-way house*
Female felon	Interview	Supervised half-way house*
Male rapist	Interview	Supervised half-way house*
Male child abuser	Interview	Supervised half-way house (men)*
Female child abuser	Interview	Supervised half-way house (women)*
Male psychopath	Diagnosis	Humane detention****
Female psychopath	Diagnosis	Humane detention****

*Includes Basic Income for all adults
**Includes Basic Income following release from treatment
***Basic Income contingent on diagnosis
****No Basic Income

tantamount to sweeping a problem under the rug, will only incur the anger of Americans who do not want troubled persons roaming their streets and forming new homeless camps. Triaging should lead to genuine solutions not perpetuating the same problems elsewhere .

OBJECTIVE #19

Decriminalize Drug Addiction

Platform holds that legal or illegal drug addiction are medical crises of the New Feudalism and should be treated as such. *Criminalization of drug addiction, like criminalization of homelessness, is a misguided national disgrace.* Legal addiction is fostered by the profiteering drug companies of the military-industrial complex; illegal addiction is fostered by profiteering drug cartels and organized crime. But in either case, the bodies and mental states of all drug addicts suffer the same incapacitating physiologic and mental dysfunctions. Drug addiction, both legal and illegal, crosses through all economic classes of the destructive New Feudalism. *Platform* holds that drug addiction is foremost a social pathology that is also causal to a medical pathology. Healing both through egalitarian intervention is essential (*page 73*). *Platform* holds further that persons arrested and incarcerated for drug use be released from all detention facilities, escorted to mandatory treatment facilities for medical evaluation and care as needed. Their eventual release back into society follows with assigned counselors and advocates for ongoing support as necessary, and conviction of drug addiction is expunged from their law enforcement records.

OBJECTIVE #20

Abortion and People's Rights

Platform concurs with the controversial 1973 Supreme Court decision, *Roe v. Wade*, which held that individual state laws banning abortion are unconstitutional. Not because *Platform* endorses or opposes abortions one way or the other, but because the government should not have the authority to supersede a person's right to determine what will, and what will not, happen medically to their own body. In the common vernacular of egalitarianism, "My body, my business. Your body, your business." States which, therefore, create legislation to prohibit abortions are violating this right of self-determination now accorded by the U.S. Constitution and should be struck down or prevented in the first place. Criticism of this right is commonly based on religious grounds or is rooted in the *male chauvin-*

ism syndrome. But the U.S. Constitution is clear that "no religious test" is going to determine our laws, and that this entrenched syndrome simply seeks to control and exploit women to its own ends. Both, however, are commonly hypocritical in their support of wars, the death penalty, blatant war crimes (atomic bombs detonated on Japanese civilians), and even torture as evidenced in Objective #16.

OBJECTIVE #21
First Amendment: Separation of Church and State

Many American Christians state that America is a Christian nation founded on Christian principles. *Platform* holds that other religions and atheists believe otherwise. In this respect, the Constitution facilitates all faiths or lack of but *favors none by law*. The First Amendment of our Bill of Rights, adopted on December 15, 1791, provides for this legal separation of church and state:

> *Congress shall make no law respecting an establishment of religion, or prohibiting the free exercise thereof;*

Thomas Jefferson's letter to the Danbury Baptist Association in 1802, assured them that the new government had no authority to prohibit "the free exercise" of their faith:

> Believing with you that religion is a matter which lies solely between Man & his God, that he owes account to none other for his faith or his worship, that the legitimate powers of government reach actions only, & not opinions, I contemplate with sovereign reverence that act of the whole American people which declared that their legislature should 'make no law respecting an establishment of religion, or prohibiting the free exercise thereof,' thus building a wall of separation between Church and State.

OBJECTIVE #22
Second Amendment: Militias vs. Right to Keep and Bear Arms

The Second Amendment to the U.S. Constitution reads:

> *A well regulated militia being necessary to the security of a free state, the right of the people to keep and bear arms shall not be infringed.*

Platform holds that the Bill of Rights Second Amendment text with its prefatory clause referring to a "well regulated militia" appears to be resolved by adjoining the necessary "right of the people to keep and bear arms" clause, which "shall not be infringed," in order to fulfill the necessity of forming state militias of those people. This continuity of clauses — in a single sentence — suggests that the authors did not intend them to be interpreted as inseparable, otherwise, common sense suggests they would have written them so. But they didn't because it would not have made sense at that time.

History shows that the formation of a federal government looming above state governments meant to many then that such an entity could arise to a tyranny over the states. Like the tyranny of King George III and his military over the colonists. Thus, well-regulated militias formed from the people would necessitate that the people be armed in order to fulfill that purpose. In fact, this was a real concern of the Constitution's authors. This is clearly stated in Alexander Hamilton's Federalist Paper No. 29, entitled, "Concerning the Militia," published on January 9, 1788. Hamilton wrote:

> ... it will be possible to have an excellent body of well-trained militia, ready to take the field whenever the defence of the State shall require it. This will not only lessen the call for military establishments, but if circumstances should at any time oblige the Government to form an army of any magnitude, that army can never be formidable to the liberties of the People, while there is a large body of citizens, little, if at all, inferior to them in discipline and the use of arms, who stand ready to defend their own rights, and those of their fellow-citizens. This appears to me the only substitute that can be devised for a standing army, and the best possible security against it, if it should exist.

The suggestion of disarming the people would then not be logical if the purpose was to have armed state militias which would also be regulated. Having just fought in the Revolutionary War, armed patriots and others living in the states were now needed to fill the ranks of the state militias. Disarming them would not make any sense. Moreover, it is certain that the same weapons would be used in hunting to feed one's family, and even to protect one's family from hostile Indians and even the ongoing military designs and intrusions of the British against the colonies, evidenced by the War of 1812. The suggestion of infringing upon the rights of people to bear arms would surely have risen to a good tavern joke in the day!

But we are now centuries later and the times have changed. Our state militias are now well-defined Guard Units under the authority of state governments, although they may be federalized if necessary to protect the nation from external or even internal threats. The secondary clause — "the right of the people to bear arms shall not be infringed" — which applied specifically to the patriots forming the militias at the time the Second Amendment became law, now deserves new clarification, because today not all people are members of the Guard Units (state militias). Thus, to whom else will the right to bear arms apply to, for what purposes, and with what restrictions? *Platform* holds that the answers should lie with the American people by popular vote — not by political proxies or special interest groups.

In recent years, a divided Supreme Court decided that the Second Amendment applies to all citizens, not just members of the militias, law enforcement, and other agencies. But with all due respect to the Court, that is the decision of just nine Americans, not all Americans by popular vote. Their decision is no more democratic than the writing of the Second Amendment itself in the first place, since only white male property owners had any say in it. The "Founding Fathers" who wrote the Constitution had it wrong on many accounts, from including the right to own slaves to preventing women from voting, as explained earlier in this book.

While it is true that millions of Americans legally own guns, and have no interest in letting others tell them to disarm and give up their guns, the same thing can be said of white Southerners in the *antebellum* U.S. who also didn't want to be told to free their black slaves. But a majority of Americans in 1861 knew better, and unfortunately it took a brutal and costly war to compel slave owners and their defenders to do the right thing. Gun owners are also a minority in the U.S. According to a 2019 Gallup poll, 70% of Americans do not own guns. A growing number of those Americans believe the Second Amendment should be repealed and re-written as a new Second Amendment that clarifies "the right to bear arms" clause independent of our regulated state militias, and that is approved by the American people by popular vote.

Most Americans, including the majority who do not own guns, would not contest a privilege (not a Constitutional right) to use guns to hunt, target practice, trade/collect/hobbies, and other recreational purposes. These activities have nothing to do with our legal law enforcement agencies, the State Guard Units (militias), and the U.S. military, all of which the vast majority of Americans respect and support. What concerns most Americans today are those individuals who obtain and use guns to break our laws and harm others. A new Second Amendment needs to address this by clarifying gun ownership, including the types of guns that Americans can use. This is important because Americans want to feel safe if there are going to be guns used at large in our society. Because if such an Amendment cannot be clarified, the American people have the right by legislation to abolish any right to private gun ownership in the U.S., just as they abolished human slavery with the 13th Amendment in 1865.

Law enforcement agencies are now prescribed to protect the people from others with criminal intent to cause harm. Militias are deployed only in extreme cases of disaster — typically environmental. But because many criminals are armed today and are murdering thousands of unarmed people every year, the suggestion by anti-gun lobbyists that citizens be disarmed and restricted from using their weapons to protect themselves, makes no more sense than disarming patriots in 1791.

Platform appreciates that resolving this clash is no simple matter. Armed and unarmed Americans on both sides want to feel safe. Many want controls put on gun access to feel safe, if necessary disarming all Americans except law enforcement. Armed Americans scoff in disbelief at this approach as being unrealistic, pointing out that criminals will continue to get their hands on guns (and other weapons) one way or the other, a claim that is really impossible to refute. It is also clear that the Second Amendment, logical in its day, is inadequate today.

Platform holds that law enforcement is probably being asked to do more than is possible in curtailing current widespread violence against the people by criminals and other disturbed persons, certainly more so in some communities than others. It may be that the role of our State Guard Units needs to be expanded to help — both as a deterrent to violent crime and through intervention. Today's Guard Units are composed of the people, just like the patriots at the dawn of the country who formed the early militias. But like the U.S. military, which they resemble in many respects, our Guard Units are largely out of sight and stay that way until called up for duty by the Governor or the U.S. President. They live among us, possibly in some of our neighborhoods, but it is more likely that we don't know who they are or where they live. In the immediate absence of law enforcement, who better prepared to step in to protect unarmed people from criminal active shooters than one's neighbors close-by who are trained and well-regulated members of our legal state militias? Arming them to augment local law enforcement, under whose authority and the Governor's they would act, would surely go a long way to making our communities safer from violent, gun-wielding criminals, rapists, and psychopaths who continue to cause great harm to Americans every year. In this way, a frustrated and fearful society avoids the scourge of vigilantism — those taking the law into their own hands — knowing that trained militia and law enforcement are in their neighborhoods working together and ready to help. Such pressure can only help to deter crime.

The question arises also out of the Second Amendment: should citizens be arming themselves in public to protect themselves (and, ostensibly, others) from persons whom they may perceive as a threat to their lives? *Platform* holds that this is a dangerous precedent that could readily evolve into vigilantism, errors in judgment, or fits of passion, as much as it could arm the criminal to commit a crime. *Platform* concurs with what would likely be a majority American decision under vote — that being armed in public is the exclusive duty and responsibility of our law enforcement agencies (including those they may legally deputize and have trained), not the average citizen.

Platform holds further that other egalitarian reforms (Objectives) can help target troubled individuals, disarm them, and get them the help they need before they cause harm to others and themselves with guns and other weapons. Concerned citizens should consider administering to these Objectives instead of arming themselves in public.

OBJECTIVE #23
Mandatory Non-Military Community Service

Non-Military Public Service ("Service" for discussion here) is a key ingredient of an egalitarian society. *Platform* holds that a two year Service would be compulsory for all 18 year olds after completing their secondary education and before pursuing careers, higher education, or entering the military or state Guard Units. The possibilities here are endless, but Service is principally centered around young adults learning to cooperate with each other in an egalitarian manner while learning about and helping communities in a variety of ways.

Assignments would be diverse with both classroom and field work, similar to the military, but serving a civilian rather than military agenda aimed at helping local communities and learning about government and private enterprise infrastructure. The Service is not a labor force to supplant workers in government or private enterprise. Further, it is a national program, so participants would not be sent to foreign countries. Examples of Service assignments:

- Organic farming and ranching
- National, state, and local parks
- Healthcare
- University and private research
- Public works
- Law enforcement
- Legal system
- Green technologies
- Food production

Service would be a conscription process similar to induction in the U.S. military, also using the Selective Service. The Service would be a federal program with cabinet level authority in the executive branch.

OBJECTIVE #24
Egalitarian Marriages

Throughout history, including the present, marriages have with relatively few exceptions been legally structured around the *male chauvinism syndrome*: men controlling women politically, economically, religiously, and by brutal force. The key word is "control." Women have had to struggle against this systematic control in the United States since the days of the Old Feudalism because of their 2nd Class legal status rooted in a flawed U.S. Constitution that facilitated political, economic, and religious discrimination against women. In effect, legal marriage meant women being the property of men. Like the African slave, also the property of men: "Marriage a prison, husbands the wardens." Worse, husbands understood that using violence to control their "difficult" woman (like a recalcitrant slave) was a duty, if not a privilege, of their wardenships. The suggestion of having to give up this authority over women sizzles the blood with rage in the mind of the male chauvinist.

Platform holds that these de facto wardenships — legally binding marriages — of the Old Feudalism are extant in the New Feudalism and should be abolished altogether. Instead marriages should be replaced by relationships based on mutual consent and respect within the context of democratic egalitarian principles and Objectives. Neither religion nor the laws would legally bind any such relationship because neither would be necessary. Thus, if one partner wishes to terminate the relationship, the other partner has no choice but to depart. Property would be divided according to previous ownership and joint ownership by mutual consent. Courts would intervene at no cost only if mutual consent cannot be arrived at. Women, living under the protective Objectives of egalitarianism, including Basic Income and home ownership — and law enforcement if necessary — would no longer be dependent on their partner to survive. They are immediately free and independent. She can return to a single life again fully protected, including her children if there are any, and look forward to the day that she will find a better partner who will truly be compatible and appreciate her. Even the most controlling prison warden, with little thought, should see the wisdom in this.

In contrast, legal marriages terminating in divorce in the New Feudalism are, with few exceptions, expensive and unpleasant affairs, especially for the burgeoning lower middle and poor classes where finances and resources are scarce. Here, women, and women with children in particular, may be left destitute with no income, homeless if public assistance housing isn't available or she has been evicted from her home or apartment, no job skills, emotional scars from being physically and mentally abused often requiring protective custody in battered women shelters (if not murdered for life insurance policies), guilt, being blamed for all that went wrong, and so forth. It is a common story told by women living in the trenches of Section 8 and other public assistance housing, and in homeless camps. This all comes to an end, however, in a democratic egalitarian society, where attorneys, judges, court bureaucrats, church elders, ex's, and others aren't needed and have no legal say or other business unless invited.

U.S. Declaration of Independence

In CONGRESS, July 4, 1776.

The unanimous Declaration of the thirteen united States of America,

When in the Course of human events, it becomes necessary for one people to dissolve the political bands which have connected them with another, and to assume among the powers of the earth, the separate and equal station to which the Laws of Nature and of Nature's God entitle them, a decent respect to the opinions of mankind requires that they should declare the causes which impel them to the separation.

We hold these truths to be self-evident, that all men are created equal, that they are endowed by their Creator with certain unalienable Rights, that among these are Life, Liberty and the pursuit of Happiness.-That to secure these rights, Governments are instituted among Men, deriving their just powers from the consent of the governed, -That whenever any Form of Government becomes destructive of these ends, it is the Right of the People to alter or to abolish it, and to institute new Government, laying its foundation on such principles and organizing its powers in such form, as to them shall seem most likely to effect their Safety and Happiness. Prudence, indeed, will dictate that Governments long established should not be changed for light and transient causes; and accordingly all experience hath shewn, that mankind are more disposed to suffer, while evils are sufferable, than to right themselves by abolishing the forms to which they are accustomed. But when a long train of abuses and usurpations, pursuing invariably the same Object evinces a design to reduce them under absolute Despotism, it is their right, it is their duty, to throw off such Government, and to provide new Guards for their future security.-Such has been the patient sufferance of these Colonies; and such is now the necessity which constrains them to alter their former Systems of Government. The history of the present King of Great Britain is a history of repeated injuries and usurpations, all having in direct object the establishment of an absolute Tyranny over these States. To prove this, let Facts be submitted to a candid world.

—He has refused his Assent to Laws, the most wholesome and necessary for the public good.

—He has forbidden his Governors to pass Laws of immediate and pressing importance, unless suspended in their operation till his Assent should be obtained; and when so suspended, he has utterly neglected to attend to them.

—He has refused to pass other Laws for the accommodation of large districts of people, unless those people would relinquish the right of Representation in the Legislature, a right inestimable to them and formidable to tyrants only.

—He has called together legislative bodies at places unusual, uncomfortable, and distant from the depository of their public Records, for the sole purpose of fatiguing them into compliance with his measures.

—He has dissolved Representative Houses repeatedly, for opposing with manly firmness his invasions on the rights of the people.

—He has refused for a long time, after such dissolutions, to cause others to be elected; whereby the Legislative powers, incapable of Annihilation, have returned to the People at large for their exercise; the State remaining in the mean time exposed to all the dangers of invasion from without, and convulsions within.

U.S. Declaration of Independence (cont'd)

—*He has endeavoured to prevent the population of these States; for that purpose obstructing the Laws for Naturalization of Foreigners; refusing to pass others to encourage their migrations hither, and raising the conditions of new Appropriations of Lands.*

—*He has obstructed the Administration of Justice, by refusing his Assent to Laws for establishing Judiciary powers.*

—*He has made Judges dependent on his Will alone, for the tenure of their offices, and the amount and payment of their salaries.*

—*He has erected a multitude of New Offices, and sent hither swarms of Officers to harrass our people, and eat out their substance.*

—*He has kept among us, in times of peace, Standing Armies without the Consent of our legislatures.*

—*He has affected to render the Military independent of and superior to the civil power.*

—*He has combined with others to subject us to a jurisdiction foreign to our constitution, and unacknowledged by our laws; giving his Assent to their Acts of pretended Legislation:*

—*For Quartering large bodies of armed troops among us:*

—*For protecting them, by a mock Trial, from punishment for any Murders which they should commit on the Inhabitants of these States:*

—*For cutting off our Trade with all parts of the world:*

—*For imposing Taxes on us without our Consent:*

—*For depriving us in many cases, of the benefits of Trial by Jury:*

—*For transporting us beyond Seas to be tried for pretended offences*

—*For abolishing the free System of English Laws in a neighbouring Province, establishing therein an Arbitrary government, and enlarging its Boundaries so as to render it at once an example and fit instrument for introducing the same absolute rule into these Colonies:*

—*For taking away our Charters, abolishing our most valuable Laws, and altering fundamentally the Forms of our Governments:*

—*For suspending our own Legislatures, and declaring themselves invested with power to legislate for us in all cases whatsoever.*

—*He has abdicated Government here, by declaring us out of his Protection and waging War against us.*

—*He has plundered our seas, ravaged our Coasts, burnt our towns, and destroyed the lives of our people.*

—*He is at this time transporting large Armies of foreign Mercenaries to compleat the works of death, desolation and tyranny, already begun with circumstances of Cruelty & perfidy scarcely paralleled in the most barbarous ages, and totally unworthy the Head of a civilized nation.*

—*He has constrained our fellow Citizens taken Captive on the high Seas to bear Arms against their Country, to become the executioners of their friends and Brethren, or to fall themselves by their Hands.*

—*He has excited domestic insurrections amongst us, and has endeavoured to bring on the inhabitants of our frontiers, the merciless Indian Savages, whose known rule of warfare, is an undistinguished destruction of all ages, sexes and conditions.*

—*In every stage of these Oppressions We have Petitioned for Redress in the most humble terms: Our repeated Petitions have been answered only by repeated injury. A Prince whose character is thus marked by every act which may define a Tyrant, is unfit to be the ruler of a free people. Nor have We been wanting in attentions to our British brethren. We have warned them from time to time of attempts by their legislature to extend an unwarrantable jurisdiction over us. We have reminded them of the circumstances of our emigra-*

U.S. Declaration of Independence (cont'd)

tion and settlement here. We have appealed to their native justice and magnanimity, and we have conjured them by the ties of our common kindred to disavow these usurpations, which, would inevitably interrupt our connections and correspondence. They too have been deaf to the voice of justice and of consanguinity. We must, therefore, acquiesce in the necessity, which denounces our Separation, and hold them, as we hold the rest of mankind, Enemies in War, in Peace Friends.

We, therefore, the **Representatives** of the **united States of America**, in General Congress, Assembled, appealing to the Supreme Judge of the world for the rectitude of our intentions, do, in the Name, and by Authority of the good People of these Colonies, solemnly publish and declare, That these United Colonies are, and of Right ought to be **Free and Independent States**, that they are Absolved from all Allegiance to the British Crown, and that all political connection between them and the State of Great Britain, is and ought to be totally dissolved; and that as Free and Independent States, they have full Power to levy War, conclude Peace, contract Alliances, establish Commerce, and to do all other Acts and Things which Independent States may of right do. And for the support of this Declaration, with a firm reliance on the protection of divine Providence, we mutually pledge to each other our Lives, our Fortunes and our sacred Honor.

Georgia
Button Gwinnett
Lyman Hall
George Walton

North Carolina
William Hooper
Joseph Hewes
John Penn

South Carolina
Edward Rutledge
Thomas Heyward, Jr.
Thomas Lynch, Jr.
Arthur Middleton

Maryland
Samuel Chase
William Paca
Thomas Stone
Charles Carroll

Virginia
George Wythe
Richard Henry Lee
Thomas Jefferson
Benjamin Harrison
Thomas Nelson, Jr.
Francis Lightfoot Lee
Carter Braxton

Pennsylvania
Robert Morris
Benjamin Rush
Benjamin Franklin
John Morton
George Clymer
James Smith
George Taylor
James Wilson
George Ross

Delaware
Caesar Rodney
George Read
Thomas McKean

New York
William Floyd
Philip Livingston
Francis Lewis
Lewis Morris

New Jersey
Richard Stockton
John Witherspoon
Francis Hopkinson
John Hart
Abraham Clark

Rhode Island
Stephen Hopkins
William Ellery

New Hampshire
Josiah Bartlett
William Whipple
Matthew Thornton

Massachusetts
Samuel Adams
John Adams
Robert Treat Paine
Elbridge Gerry
John Hancock

Connecticut
Roger Sherman
Samuel Huntington
William Williams
Oliver Wolcott

Index of Objectives

Attributions

Cover (front/back)
- Flag: Lukas Gojda © www.123rf.com
- All other images see below pages 17, 23, 27, 47, 50.

Title page
- Tommie Stevens

P.9 (facing page)
- Public Domain

P. 12
- Public Domain

P. 13
- Public Domain

P. 14
- South Africa The Good News / www.sagoodnews.co.za

P. 17
- Public Domain: Based on Larry Bartels's study Economic Inequality and Political Representation, Table 1: Differential Responsiveness of Senators to Constituency Opinion.
- Original color transparency of FDR taken at 1944 Official Campaign Portrait session by Leon A. Perskie, Hyde Park, New York, August 21, 1944. Gift of Beatrice Perskie Foxman and Dr. Stanley B. Foxman. August 21, 1944

P. 18
- © O'Dea at Wikimedia Commons, CC BY-SA 4.0

P. 19
- https://commons.wikimedia. org/wiki/File:Street_Sleeper_3_ by_David_Shankbone.JPG

P. 21
- Public Domain: https:// hiddenhillscity.org/

P. 23
- Public Domain: Digital image ©1998 Missouri Historical Society, St. Louis. Dred Scott (1795 – 1858), plaintiff in the infamous Dred Scott v. Sandford (1857) case at the Supreme Court of the United States, commissioned by a "group of Negro citizens" and presented to the Missouri Historical Society, St. Louis, in 1888.

P. 25
- https://commons.wikimedia. org/wiki/File:Military_Road _ Marker_US_64_Marion _AR. jpg
- Public Domain

P. 27-41
- Public Domain

P. 43
- Public Domain: https://www. gnu.org/licenses/old-licenses/ fdl-1.2.html: SLOWKING

P. 45-50
- Public Domain

P. 51
- Jaime Jackson

P. 53
- Public Domain: US incarceration timeline-clean.svg

P. 59-68
- Public Domain

P. 72
- https://commons.wikimedia. org/wiki/File:Man_sleeping_ on_ Canadian_sidewalk.jpg — The Blackbird (Jay Black) [CC BY-SA 2.0 (https://creative commons.org/licenses/by-sa/2.0)]

P. 73
- Jaime Jackson

P. 87
- Jill Willis

About the Author

I've always been a maverick thinker and doer, never satisfied with life's limits as I've perceived them to be in the mainstream. For example, after leaving the U.S. Army in early 1970 with an honorable discharge, I joined other veterans in the antiwar movement in protest of the corporate "war for profits" in Vietnam and the average American's unwitting complicity. "No business as usual" was our mantra, and on many fronts the burgeoning protest movement confronted every institution across the country. As mounting numbers of dead and wounded were returned home, the entire nation began questioning and then demanding an end to the war. In 1975 President Nixon felt the hand of the movement and shut it down — the greatest military blunder in the history of the U.S. After that, we all went own separate ways.

My calling became "nature" and what we can learn as a species from our natural world, past and present. My books continue to tell my own story, where I've gone, what I've got myself into, with whom, and why. *Platform* is one chapter in that story.